Bible Stories from the
NEW
TESTAMENT

Bible Stories from the
NEW TESTAMENT

Written by Patricia Hunt

Illustrated by Angus McBride

CRESCENT BOOKS · NEW YORK

© Text Patricia Hunt 1983
© Illustrations Ward Lock Limited 1983

First published in Great Britain in 1983
by Ward Lock Limited, 8 Clifford Street,
London W1X 1RB, an Egmont Company

This 1984 edition is published by
Crescent Books, distributed by
Crown Publishers, Inc.
HGFEDCB
ISBN 0-517-439107
Printed and bound in Czechoslovakia

Contents

The Birth of Jesus

In the little town of Nazareth in Galilee there lived a good and gentle young woman named Mary. She was engaged to a local carpenter named Joseph, a fine, kindly man whose family was descended from King David.

One day, as Mary went about her household duties, she had a surprising visitor. An angel named Gabriel suddenly appeared before her. 'Hail, Mary,' he said, 'the Lord is with you.'

Mary was puzzled, for she did not understand what the angel's visit could mean.

'Do not be afraid, Mary,' said the angel, 'for you are to have a son, and His name will be Jesus. He will be the son of the Most High God, and He will be a king whose kingdom will never end.'

'How can this be?' asked Mary, greatly worried. 'I have no husband.'

'The Holy Spirit will come to you,' answered the angel, 'so that God's power will be with you, for the child will be the Son of God.'

This was amazing news, but the angel had more to say. 'Your relation, Elizabeth, is also going to have a son,' he went on, 'although she is thought to be too old to have any children now. With God nothing is impossible.'

'I am God's servant,' said Mary quietly. 'May it happen as you have said.'

And then the angel left her.

Shortly afterwards, Mary went to visit her cousin Elizabeth, and when she told her the news,

Elizabeth said, 'You are the most blessed of women! Why should such a wonderful thing happen that the mother of the Lord should visit me?'

Joseph, however, was troubled at Mary's news and wondered whether he should still marry her. Then an angel appeared to him in a dream and reassured him, 'Do not be afraid to take Mary for your wife. God's Holy Spirit has come to her, and she will have a son who is to be called Jesus—for He will save people from their sins.'

(The name 'Jesus' is in fact the Greek form of the Hebrew name 'Joshua' and means 'saviour').

Bethlehem

Now Palestine in those days was part of the Roman Empire, and some time after the appearance of the angel to Mary and Joseph, the Roman Emperor, Caesar Augustus, issued an order. He commanded that everyone should be 'enrolled', which meant that there would be a sort of census or numbering of the people. To do this, each person was to return to his home town or city to register himself.

For Joseph this meant a long journey of about 115 km (72 miles), from Nazareth in Galilee southwards to Bethlehem in Judea. Bethlehem had been the home of Ruth and Boaz, and also the birthplace of King David.

The journey would be a long and tiring walk, for, apart from a donkey, there was no other means of transport. Joseph had to make careful preparations for the journey, especially as Mary was going with him and would soon be having her baby.

They were both very tired by the time they reached Bethlehem. What a busy town it was! Everywhere was hustle and bustle, for crowds of people had come for the enrolment. There seemed to be no room anywhere for the weary travellers from Bethlehem to stay the night. Joseph was anxious about Mary, and became worried when the last innkeeper they asked told him that he had not a single room left vacant in the inn; he was completely full with visitors.

Then, no doubt, he looked again at Mary and saw how tired she was, and he took pity on her. 'There is the stable where the animals are kept,' he suggested. 'You could shelter there for the night if you wish.'

Joseph was ready to take anything, for he could see that Mary was not fit to travel much further, and he readily agreed. At least the stable would provide shelter, and they could find a warm corner and lie down on some of the animals' straw.

Thankfully, they went into the stable, and during the night, with no one looking on except the animals, Mary's baby was born. She wrapped Him up in strips of cloth, called swaddling clothes, which was the usual custom in that part of the world. There was no cradle where she might lay her baby, so she put Him gently in a manger where hay was kept to feed the animals.

It was a strange arrival for the Son of God. Kings are not normally born in stables; they are born in palaces amid rich pomp and splendour, but when God allowed Jesus to be born in this humble way in the stable, He was showing that He was sympathetic to the poor and was the king of *all* people, not only of the rich and important. By living as the poorest, Jesus would show how He really understood them and took their part.

In the countryside, outside Bethlehem, a group of shepherds were looking after their sheep on the night when Jesus was born.

The work of shepherds was important and dangerous, since not only had they to lead their flocks to pasture, they had also to protect them from any wild animals that came prowling around. To this end, they stayed with their sheep both day and night, and when the flock was herded into the fold, often the shepherd himself would lie across the opening of the doorway, so that nothing could get into the pen without his knowledge.

On this clear night, the Bethlehem shepherds wrapped their cloaks around them against the cold and talked among themselves. Perhaps they remembered that King David had once been a shepherd boy himself. They gazed up at the night sky and saw many bright stars, but they were used to that.

Suddenly there seemed to be much more light than usual. The whole field was lit up with a brilliant radiance, and in the midst of it the shepherds saw the figure of an angel. They were terrified and covered their faces.

'Do not be afraid' said the angel, 'for I have brought you good news; news which will bring great joy to all the people. This very day in Bethlehem, the city of David, the Saviour of the world has been born. He is Christ the Lord.'

The shepherds were amazed; they could hardly take in such an important announcement and naturally they wondered why the angel had come to them with this great news.

The angel continued, 'As a sign to prove it to you, you will find the baby wrapped in swaddling clothes and lying in a manger.'

Hardly had the angel's words died away, than the whole sky surrounding the spot was filled with a multitude of angels. 'Glory to God in the highest,' they sang, 'and on earth peace to men with whom He is pleased.'

Then the angels went away, and the earth grew quiet and still. Only the stars were left in the sky.

The shepherds looked at one another in wonder. Was it true? Could they be dreaming? The Messiah, the Saviour of the world, here in Bethlehem? and in a *stable*? It did not seem possible.

Then one of the shepherds said, 'Come on, let's go and see this wonderful thing which the Lord has told us about through His angel.'

They hurried off, over the hills, and into Bethlehem. Almost certainly they left one of their number behind to take care of the sheep.

But where in Bethlehem should they look? From what the angel had said, the shepherds knew that it would be useless to look in any rich or important house, for the baby would be lying in a manger. Any rich house would provide a proper cot. Mangers were found only in stables, so they must look for a stable if they wanted to find the new-born king.

When at last they looked in at the stable belonging to the inn, there they found the new baby, and they knelt down and worshipped Him in wonder.

Mary, His mother, and Joseph, her husband, were gazing fondly down at Him. The shepherds told them all that the angel had said, but Mary already knew something about her wonderful baby, for the angel Gabriel had told her whom He was to be. So she kept silent, but thought a great deal about the wonderful happening.

The shepherds, however, were greatly excited about the event, and they could not keep quiet about it. They returned to their sheep, singing praises to God. They had heard the angel with their own ears, they had seen the baby with their own eyes; however much other people might find it hard to believe that God's Son had been born in a stable, they knew that it was true.

Forty days after Jesus was born, Mary and Joseph, according to the law, took Him to the temple in Jerusalem to be presented to God. On these occasions, it was necessary to present an offering, which would normally be a lamb. Poor people, however, such as Mary and Joseph, were allowed to offer two turtle-doves or two young pigeons instead.

In Jerusalem at that time, there lived a good man whose name was Simeon. He was a God-fearing man, and it had been revealed to him that he would not die until he had seen the true Christ. ('Christ' comes from a Greek word meaning 'anointed'; and 'Messiah' from a Hebrew word meaning the same thing.) It happened that he was in the temple when Mary and Joseph came in to present Jesus. As soon as Simeon saw Jesus he knew who He was and came forward at once.

Simeon took the baby in his arms and said, 'Lord, now let your servant go in peace, for I have seen the Saviour with my own eyes.'

Mary and Joseph were amazed at the things which Simeon said, for they were only slowly realizing the wonderful truth about their baby. Simeon blessed them too, and then he told Mary that Jesus would be the salvation of many in Israel, but that many people would speak against Him, and that she would suffer much sorrow.

The Visit of the Wise Men

Some time after the birth of Jesus, a group of rather important-looking men arrived in Jerusalem and began asking questions. They were men who studied the stars and their meanings, and were known as astrologers, or sometimes as 'magi', or just 'wise men'.

They had come on a long journey from the east, from where, before they had begun their travels, they had seen a very bright new star in the sky. From their knowledge, they believed that this star meant the birth of the long-promised new King of the Jews. So, wanting to find out more, they had set off on their camels to follow the star. (The Bible does not say that there were three of them, but it has always been generally thought that this was so because they brought three gifts.)

When the star had led them as far as Jerusalem, the wise men began to ask people if this was the place to which they should come to find the new king. Surely Jerusalem was a suitable place for a king to be born, they thought. 'Where is He who is born King of the Jews?' they asked. 'We have seen His star in the east, and have travelled here to worship Him.'

But no one in Jerusalem knew anything about a king being born there. So far as they knew, the only king in the area was Herod.

The news about the wise men's questionings reached the ears of King Herod, and he did not like the sound of it at all. He was a very jealous character, and he wanted no rivals to his throne or his power.

'A new king?' he thought, and became full of mistrust and suspicion. Not only was he troubled, but all the people of Jerusalem were troubled too, for when Herod was upset one never knew what he might do. He had killed many of the leading men of the city not long before, while suffering from a fit of fear and jealousy. He really could not be trusted an inch.

Herod summoned together all the chief priests and teachers of the law and asked them what they knew about it. 'Where will this Messiah, this King of the Jews, be born?' he asked in a pleasant, interested way.

They knew the answer to that one. It had been foretold by the prophet Micah hundreds of years earlier. He had written, 'And you, Bethlehem, in the land of Judah, are not the least of the cities of Judah, for from you there will come a ruler who will guide the people of Israel.' That could only mean the Messiah.

'Bethlehem,' thought Herod. 'Something must be done about this without delay.' So he summoned the wise men from the east to a secret conference. He found out from them at what time the star had appeared, and then he sent them off to Bethlehem to look for the new king whose birth seemed such a threat to him.

'Go and search very carefully for the young child,' he told them, 'and as soon as you have found him, come back here and let me know; for I would like to go and worship him too.' Of course, Herod had no intention of going to worship a rival king. All he wanted was to find out where the child was so that he could have him removed as a rival to the throne and make sure that he, Herod, was the only king the Jews recognized.

The wise men left Jerusalem. They were pleased to see the star again and to follow it until it came to

rest over Bethlehem, and over a certain house there. Now that the enrolling and the census was over, Bethlehem was no longer full of visitors, and Mary and Joseph would have had no difficulty in finding somewhere better than a stable to live in and to bring up the new baby.

Joyfully the wise men went into the house where they saw the young child Jesus and His mother, and they knelt down and worshipped Him, happy that their long search was over.

Then, as it was the custom not to approach a monarch without bringing a gift, they presented their gifts to the new King of the Jews. They were royal gifts—of gold, frankincense and myrrh—costly products of the countries from which the men had come. Frankincense was the resin from the bark of the terebinth tree; it had a pleasant smell and was used by priests in temple worship to make fragrant smoke at the altar. Myrrh was a sweet-smelling gum and was used as a perfume, in medicine and in anointing oils. They were all most suitable gifts for a king.

While in Bethlehem the wise men had a dream, which through their learning they were able to interpret, and in it God warned them not to go back to King Herod, as he had requested; so they went back home another way, slipping quietly across the borders of Israel.

When the wise men did not return to Jerusalem, Herod realized that he had been tricked, and he flew into a furious rage. He gave orders that all baby boys in Bethlehem, who were two years old

and under, were to be killed at once. That way, he thought, he would be sure to kill the new king among them.

Meanwhile, after the wise men had departed, Joseph also had a dream in which an angel appeared to him and said, 'Get up quickly, and take the young child, and Mary His mother, and escape into Egypt, for King Herod is looking for the child in order to kill Him.'

So that night, under cover of darkness, Joseph did as the angel had bidden him, and with Mary and Jesus he fled into Egypt, out of the range of Herod's power. So Herod's wicked plot was foiled, and there they remained until the day that Herod died.

Then the angel appeared to Joseph in another dream and said, 'It is quite safe for you to take the child and His mother back to Israel now, for those who were searching for Him, to kill Him, are themselves now dead.'

At first Joseph thought of returning to Judah, perhaps to Bethlehem, but when he heard that Archelaus was now king there, in place of his father Herod, he was afraid, for Archelaus was nearly as suspicious and cruel as his father had been. So Joseph went instead to Galilee and there he, Mary and Jesus settled in Nazareth which lay in lower Galilee on the slopes of the Lebanon mountain range. Like Bethlehem it too was a quite unimportant town that was never to be forgotten because of its links with Jesus. And so it was in Nazareth that Jesus spent His boyhood.

Jesus as a Boy

Jesus was to live in Nazareth until He was about thirty years old, and this is why, although He was born in Bethlehem, He is often known as Jesus of Nazareth. The Bible tells us that He 'increased in wisdom and stature, and in favour with God and man.' In other words, He grew, not only in height, but also in wisdom, knowledge and learning, and with God's blessing, and people loved Him and respected Him.

As a boy, He would help Mary in the everyday tasks of their humble home and also work with Joseph in making articles of wood in their carpenter's shop. There He would become a skilled worker in wood, learning to make roofs, doors, beds, chests, tables and chairs. Carpenters also made agricultural implements, such as ploughs, yokes and threshing instruments, so there would be plenty to keep the boy Jesus busy in the small farming community.

He would also be taught in the local synagogue by the rabbi or scribes, where He would learn about the Jewish law. There would be no books, and education consisted chiefly of repeating words and so learning the facts by heart. Every Sabbath He would attend the synagogue for worship, and when He grew up, He would read aloud the scriptures there as would Joseph and all the other boys and their fathers.

In His free time, He probably wandered about the countryside, where many of the things He saw, He remembered and used later in His teaching when He grew up and told people stories, or parables, about the familiar things of life—cornfields, sowers, vineyards, sheep and shepherds. His own knowledge made the stories very real and appealing to His listeners and helped them to see how the stories made sense in their own lives and dealt with their common problems.

Every year Mary and Joseph used to journey to Jerusalem to join with hundreds of other pilgrims who flocked there from all over Palestine to celebrate the Passover.

When a Jewish boy was twelve years of age, he had to undergo preparation to become an adult in the religious community and to take his full part in the religious life of the village. He would then become what was known as a 'son of the law' and be expected to obey its rules. From that time onward, he would no longer be looked upon as a child, but would be considered as a full member of the Jewish church.

So, when Jesus was twelve, Mary and Joseph decided that the time had come for Him to go with them on their visit to the festival at Jerusalem. Because of all that it meant, it would be a very special visit for Jesus.

People from the same town or village would often make the journey together, walking along the rough highways and sleeping out at nights on the way. They travelled in groups for safety, for there were robbers and other possible dangers. It was a long journey, and they would be on the road for several days. The young boys would find it a very exciting adventure, and would be thrilled when they saw Jerusalem for the first time. They would then take part in ceremonies which they would remember all their lives.

When the festival was over the people started to walk back home again, but on this particular occasion, Jesus stayed behind in Jerusalem, and

did not set off back with His parents, although they did not realize this. No doubt they thought He was somewhere in the great company of people walking back—perhaps with relatives or friends, or with other boys of His own age, racing on ahead, or stopping to explore.

After they had been walking for a day, they made an evening halt, and it was then that Mary and Joseph found that Jesus was nowhere to be seen in the company. Where could He be? Anxiously they asked around among the other travellers, but no one could recall seeing Him that day. Mary and Joseph became very worried and decided that the best thing to do was to retrace their steps to Jerusalem, in the hope that they would find him on the way.

The next day, they set off back to the city, asking everyone they met whether they had seen

Jesus, but no one could help them. At last they reached Jerusalem itself and began looking in the city. It was now three days since they had started out on the homeward journey. After much worried searching, they finally found Jesus in the temple itself. He was sitting with a group of Jewish teachers, listening to them and asking them questions. The teachers were amazed at Jesus's understanding and at His intelligent questions and answers.

Mary and Joseph, too, were astonished when they discovered where Jesus was and what He was doing. Mary said to Him, 'My son, why did you stay behind like this? Why have you treated us so? We have been most worried trying to find you.'

Jesus was surprised—not that they had come back for Him, but at their not knowing where He would be. He had thought they would have known He would be in the temple. 'Why did you need to look for me?' He asked. 'Did you not know that I had to be in My Father's house and about My Father's business?'

By His 'Father', He meant God; for even at that early age, He understood His special relationship with God the Father.

Mary and Joseph did not fully understand His answer, but Jesus then went back to Nazareth with them, and was obedient to them, thus showing His love and respect for them both.

Mary thought deeply about what had happened. She remembered the words of the angel Gabriel before Jesus was born, that her child was to be the Son of God; and also how the aged Simeon in the temple had called Jesus 'the Saviour'. She must have wondered what the future had in store.

John the Baptist

Some little time before Jesus was born, there lived an old priest of the temple named Zechariah (sometimes written Zacharia). His wife was named Elizabeth and she was related to Mary, Jesus's mother. Both were good people, obeying God's laws, but they did not have any children and would have liked one very much. They had prayed for a child, but felt they were now too old.

Once a year Zechariah had to go to the temple at Jerusalem for two weeks to carry out his special duties as a priest. In this particular year, he received an honour which only occurred once in a lifetime. He was chosen to offer the incense in the temple, the most solemn part of the day's service. It was done every morning and evening on the golden altar of incense which stood before the veil of the Holy of Holies inside the temple.

The priest, whose duty and privilege it was, went alone within the temple to offer the incense, and the other priests and people worshipped outside in the temple courts during the hour when the incense was burnt.

As Zechariah was doing his turn of duty, he suddenly looked up and saw an angel at the right-hand side of the altar. He was alarmed and afraid at this strange sight.

'Don't be afraid, Zechariah,' said the angel, 'God has heard your prayers and you and Elizabeth will have a son. You will name him John and he will be a great man in God's sight, filled with the Holy Spirit. How happy you and many others will be when he is born! He will go before the Lord, full of power, like the mighty prophet Elijah. He will prepare the way for the coming of the Lord.'

'But I am an old man,' said Zechariah, 'and my wife is old too. How can I know that what you say is so?'

'I am Gabriel,' the angel answered, 'I stand in God's presence, and it is He who has sent me to bring you this good news. However, since you have not believed me you will remain dumb, unable to speak, until the day when these things which God has promised come true.'

Meanwhile, the people were waiting outside for Zechariah to come out of the temple, and they were wondering why he took so long.

When at last he did come out, he was unable to speak and to give the people his priestly blessing; he could only make signs to them, and so they realized that something had happened to him in the temple.

In due time, Elizabeth had a baby boy, just as God had promised through the angel. All her relatives and friends were delighted that God had been so good to her and had sent her a son in her old age, and they all rejoiced with her.

The time came for the baby to be given his name. Everyone thought he would be called Zechariah after his father, and they were very surprised when Elizabeth shook her head and said, 'No, he is going to be named John.'

'John?' queried the relatives and friends. 'But why? There is no one in your family called by that name.' Then they made signs to Zechariah, who was still dumb, asking him what he would like the baby to be called. Zechariah signalled back, asking for a writing tablet and, when it was brought to him, he wrote on it, 'His name is John.'

Immediately he found he was dumb no longer and could speak again.

This made a great impression on the people, and they were full of fear at what had happened. They all talked about it to everyone they met, and the news soon spread through all the hill country of Judea. People said to one another, 'What is this child going to be? It is plain that the power of God is with him.'

As the boy John grew up he lived in the desert until the time came for him to begin his special work as a prophet among the people of Israel; the work for which God had sent him.

He was a strange, rugged-looking man, dressed in a garment made of cloth woven from camel's hair, with a leather belt round his waist. His food was strange too, for he ate locusts and wild honey. In that land the poorer people often ate locusts, after the wings and legs had been removed and the remaining parts either boiled or roasted. Honey was plentiful in the desert, being found in honey-combs in the crevices of rocks.

Out of the desert came John, a stern, fiery prophet, calling upon the people to repent, to turn away from their sins and to begin a new way of life, because the Kingdom of God was near. News of him travelled fast, and crowds flocked to hear this strange new preacher. They came from Jerusalem and from all the surrounding country of Judea.

'Prepare the way of the Lord,' cried John. 'Make a straight path for Him; fill up the valleys and level off the hill-tops; make the crooked places straight and the rough places smooth. Then every-one will see God's salvation.'

This was a colourful way of saying, 'Get rid of unbelief and the things you have neglected to do (valleys); fill the spaces with new grace; get rid of pride and haughtiness (hills), cast them down and become humble; straighten out all deceit and

untruthfulness (crooked places), and get rid of anger, hatred and malice (rough places).'

'Confess your sins, be truly sorry and come and be baptized,' called John, and hundreds of people came out to be baptized in the River Jordan. Being baptized meant being 'washed' and was a symbol of the cleaning up of the previous life— a sign that all earlier wrongs were washed away and that a new and better life could be started. Because of this baptizing work, John came to be known as John the Baptist. ·

Many of the people thought that, because they were Jews, they were better than other people, but John would have none of this. He told the Jews that they needed to repent and to confess their sins, just like everyone else. 'You must do the things which will show that you have turned away from your sins and intend to lead a new life,' John told them.

'What shall we do, then?' the people asked.

'Show your intentions by your deeds,' said John. 'If you have two coats, give one to someone who has none. If you have food, see that you share it.'

'What about us?' asked some tax-collectors.

'Do not take any more money from people than the legal amount which you are supposed to take,' said John.

'And what shall we do?' asked some soldiers.

'Do not rob anyone by force,' said John, 'and do not accuse anyone of something which you know is not true. Be content with your wages.'

Not surprisingly, people began to wonder about this new prophet. Was he perhaps the expected Messiah? The Jewish authorities in Jerusalem sent some priests and Levites to ask John who he was.

But John answered, 'No, I am not the Messiah. I baptize with water, but there is One coming who is much greater than I am. I am not even good enough to untie His sandals. He will baptize you with the Holy Spirit and with fire.' By 'fire' John meant 'holy fervour and zeal in God's service'.

The next day John saw Jesus coming towards him. John pointed Him out to the people and said, 'Look, there He is! That is the One who will take away the sins of the world. It was He whom I was talking about when I said there was One coming who was much greater than me. I did not know who He was, but I came to baptize you with water, so that He might be known to the people of Israel.'

John called Jesus 'the Lamb of God'. This is a phrase which comes from Old Testament sacrifices. Sin meant that people were separated from God and therefore under a death-sentence. In Old Testament days it was customary to offer, as a sacrifice, the death of an animal in place of the death of a person, and often this was a lamb. But when Jesus came, He came to save the world. He was to die, giving His life once and for all, on behalf of sinners, just like a lamb being sacrificed for human sin.

John was very surprised when Jesus came forward to the river to be baptized and felt that this was something which he could not do. Surely Jesus should be baptizing him instead, he thought. So he tried to prevent Jesus from being baptized, but Jesus told him it was God's will.

John agreed, and went into the river with Jesus to baptize Him. People went right into the water to be baptized in those days, and this is still done today in many places with warm climates.

As soon as Jesus came up out of the river, it seemed that the heavens opened, and John saw the Holy Spirit in the form of a dove, come down and alight on Jesus. At the same time a voice from heaven was heard saying, 'This is My beloved Son, with whom I am well pleased.'

These words showed that the baptism of Jesus did not mean that Jesus was a sinner who needed baptizing to wash away former sins like everyone else. God's words showed that Jesus was without sin but that He was now ready to identify Himself with all men and to take on the responsibility for their sin.

Temptation in the Wilderness

After Jesus's baptism by John, God led Him into the desert where He was tempted by the Devil. Jesus was in the desert for forty days and nights, during which time He did not eat any food. He was preparing for, and thinking much about the work which He was to do. How should He use His God-given powers? To satisfy His own needs? To compel people to follow Him? No, this was not the way. He knew that His power must serve men, who must only come to follow Him through their own free will. No one can be forced into the Kingdom of Heaven.

In the first temptation which came to Him from the Devil, the Devil asked Jesus, 'If you are really God's Son, command these stones to be turned into bread.' He knew that Jesus had not eaten for a long time and must be hungry, and that therefore it would be a temptation to use His powers to aid Himself.

Jesus replied, 'The scripture says, "Man shall not live by bread alone, but by every word which God speaks".' He meant that 'Since I am here by God's command, He will keep me alive without bread. I trust Him.'

Then the Devil tried a second temptation. He took Jesus to the highest point of the temple in Jerusalem and said, 'If you are God's Son, throw yourself down from the top here; you will be quite safe for the scriptures say that the angels will take care of you so that you won't be hurt on the stones.'

This was a temptation to take a short, easy and spectacular way to being recognized as the Messiah, by falling, unharmed, to the ground from a great height. Again the Devil craftily quoted scripture to support this temptation.

But Jesus firmly rejected this idea saying, 'The scripture also says, "Do not put God to the test."'

He did not want people to follow Him just because they were astounded at His miracles, but rather because they were truly attracted to His life and teaching, and by the love of God which was shown in all that He said and did. He knew that was the only way in which their faith would become deep and lasting.

Then the Devil had a third try. He took Jesus to the top of a very high mountain, from where he showed Him all the kingdoms of the world. 'All these', he said, 'I will give to you, if only you will worship me.'

The Devil wanted Jesus to acknowledge him and to do evil for the sake of becoming rich and powerful.

Jesus gave him a plain, straightforward answer 'Go away. The scripture says, "Worship the Lord your God, and serve Him only."'

After this, the Devil gave up his hopeless task and left Jesus alone.

The Twelve Disciples

Now Jesus was ready to begin His work, and to do this He chose a band of twelve men to help Him. They were quite ordinary people, whom He knew would be capable of great things.

One day, at about four o'clock in the afternoon, John the Baptist was with two of his followers when he saw Jesus walking by. 'There He is!' John pointed out. 'That is the Lamb of God.'

One of the two men was named Andrew. When he and the other man heard what John said, they went after Jesus, and Jesus turned and saw them.

'What are you looking for?' He asked.

'Where do you live, teacher?' they asked Him.

'Come and see,' said Jesus; so they went with Him, saw where He was living, and spent the rest of the day with Him.

Andrew was so impressed with Jesus that he immediately went and found his own brother,

Simon. 'Simon, we have found the Messiah,' he said, and he took Simon to Jesus.

Jesus looked at Simon and saw what was in him. He knew what a great leader this man could be, and He said, 'From now on you will be called Cephas' (which means 'a rock' and is the same word as 'Peter'. This is why Simon is often referred to as 'Simon Peter' or simply as 'Peter'). Because Andrew brought his brother to Jesus, he was really the first Christian missionary.

Both Andrew and Simon Peter were simple fishermen. They worked in their fishing business with two other brothers whose names were James and John, and whose father was named Zebedee. James and John became disciples too, and three of these first four (Peter, James and John) were to become specially close to Jesus.

After this first call, these four attached themselves to Jesus as disciples, or learners, and when they realized that He was the Messiah, they were ready to leave their homes, their business and everything, and to follow Him completely.

It happened that Jesus was walking along the shores of the Sea of Galilee one day when He again saw the fishermen at their work. (The Lake or Sea of Galilee was also called the Sea of Tiberias because the town of Tiberias lay on its western shore. It is a low, freshwater lake, measuring some 21 km [13 miles] long by about 11 km [6½ miles] wide. Much of Jesus's ministry was to take place in the towns and countryside around the lake, in places like Capernaum and Bethsaida.)

The people were crowding around Jesus, wanting to hear what He had to say about God and His

Kingdom. Jesus saw two boats pulled up to the shore, one of which belonged to Simon Peter. He got into it and asked Simon to push it out a little way so that He could sit in it and teach the people on the shore. They could all see and hear Him more easily that way.

When He had finished speaking, He said to Simon Peter, 'Push your boat out further into the deep water and then let down your nets for a catch.'

'But master,' said Simon, 'we have been out all night and have caught nothing. Still, if You say so, we will obey.'

When the fishermen let down their nets they caught such a great number of fish that the nets were almost broken with the weight. They had to signal to their partners in the other boat to come and help them. Both boats were soon so full of fish that they were about to sink.

Simon Peter was so impressed that he felt himself much too unworthy to remain in the presence of such a powerful person as Jesus. He said to Jesus, 'Depart from me, for I am a sinful man.'

'Don't be afraid,' said Jesus, 'for from now on, all your life you will be catching people not fish.'

On another day, when Jesus was in Galilee, He called a man named Philip to follow Him. Philip came from Bethsaida, the place where Andrew and Simon Peter lived, and he brought another future disciple, Nathanael, also sometimes called Bartholomew, to Jesus.

'We have found the one whom Moses and the prophets wrote about,' Philip told Nathanael. 'He is Jesus, the son of Joseph, from Nazareth.'

Nathanael was doubtful. 'Can anything good come from Nazareth?' he asked.

To which Philip replied simply, 'Come and see.'

When Jesus saw Nathanael coming towards Him, He said that here was an honest and true Israelite.

'How do you know me?' asked Nathanael, and Jesus replied that He had seen Nathanael under a fig-tree before Philip had even called him. Nathanael was quite astonished.

Another time Jesus saw a man who was a tax-collector sitting in his tax office, and said to him, 'Follow me,' and the man followed Him. He was Matthew, also called Levi. Tax-collectors, or publicans, who collected taxes on behalf of the Romans were much despised as they often took more money than they were entitled to. But Jesus did not despise anyone, and He always had a special care for those who were despised and outcast by others.

The full list of the inner band of twelve is— Simon Peter, Andrew, James, John, Philip, Nathanael, Matthew, Thomas, another James (son of Alphaeus), Thaddaeus, another Simon (the Zealot), and Judas Iscariot.

A Wedding at Cana

This is the story, from St John's Gospel, of the first miracle which Jesus performed.

One day there was to be a wedding in the little town of Cana in Galilee, a few kilometres north-east of Nazareth. Jesus, His mother, Mary, and His disciples had all been invited to the feast to celebrate the happy occasion and to offer their best wishes to their friends.

The bride's friends and the female members of her house had to get the bride ready for the ceremony, and to see that she appeared at her very best before the bridegroom. During the evening of the day of the marriage, the bridegroom and his friends would go to the bride's house; then he would take her back to his or his parents' house for the wedding supper. The marriage feast itself was usually held at the bridegroom's house, and all the relatives and friends were invited. It was considered an insult to refuse such an invitation. The wedding was a joyful occasion which lasted several days, and there was plenty of music, laughter and fun.

At the wedding in Cana, where Jesus and His mother were present, an embarrassing thing happened. The supply of wine ran out long before the guests had had enough!

Jesus's mother saw what had happened, and she did as she must have done many a time; she went and told Jesus about it. 'They have no wine left,' she said.

No one knew much about Jesus as yet, for so far He had not performed any miracles, but Mary must have thought that if anyone could do anything to help, then her son could.

Jesus replied gently and respectfully to His mother, 'I am not concerned as you are. My time has not yet come.'

Mary may not have fully understood what Jesus meant by this, but she went over to the servants and said, 'Do whatever Jesus tells you to do.'

Now the Jews had special rules and customs about washing, particularly about washing their hands before eating, and the water for this was put into large stone waterpots. At the wedding at Cana there were six of these large pots, each of which could hold about 100 litres (22 gal). They stood in a corner, out of the way.

Jesus went to the servants and said, 'Fill the jars with water.' This must have sounded a strange thing to do when the feast was short of wine, but the servants remembered Mary's instructions, and so they obeyed and filled the jars right up to the brim.

Then Jesus said to them, 'Now draw some of the water out and take it over to the steward of the feast.'

The steward was usually a friend of the bridegroom and was in charge of the running of the feast—a sort of master of ceremonies. He must have been very worried at what had occurred, and was no doubt wondering whatever he could do to help the bridegroom out of such an embarrassing situation.

He had not seen what had happened with the water jars, but he took what he thought was the water which the servants brought him, tasted it, and found that it was the very best wine. He had no idea where this very superior wine could have come from. The servants knew, and Mary knew,

A Wedding at Cana

A Wedding at Cana

but probably very few of the other people there were aware of what had happened because they were so busy having a good time.

The steward called the bridegroom over to him and said, 'Everyone else serves the best wine first, and then, if any more is needed, the more ordinary wine is served. But you have kept the best wine until now!'

After the wedding was over, Jesus and His mother, His brothers and His disciples went to Capernaum for a few days.

In this way Jesus performed His first miracle. It was not connected to serious illness or a great disaster, but was a simple act of kindness, done so that people's happiness should not be spoiled.

The Wise and Foolish Maidens

Later Jesus was to use the idea of a wedding in one of the stories He told to explain His second coming and the Day of Judgment.

One of these was about ten young girls, friends of a bride, who went out to meet the bridegroom and bring him in to the wedding feast.

Night was falling and each of the girls took a small lamp with her to light the way. Five of the girls were prudent enough to take extra oil along as fuel for their lamps, but the other five did not think of this.

The girls had to wait a long time for the bridegroom and one by one the lamps of the five thoughtless girls ran out of oil. At last they were forced to leave the group and go to find more oil for their lamps.

In their absence the bridegroom arrived and went to the feast with the five girls who were still waiting for him.

When the others eventually came back they were too late and were unable to join the feast.

Jesus said that He was like the bridegroom for whose arrival mankind should always be prepared.

The Death of John the Baptist

One day Jesus and His disciples were in the country districts of Judea. Further north, at about the same time, John the Baptist was baptizing people at a place named Aenon near Salim—a place where there was plenty of water for John to carry out his work.

People were coming from far and near to John and to Jesus, and it so happened that more people went to Jesus than went to John. This made some of John's disciples jealous and they went to John and said, 'You remember the man whom you pointed out when you were beyond Jordan? Now He is baptizing too and everyone is going to Him instead of coming here.'

Many leaders would have been angry or jealous to hear news like this, but John did not show any bitterness or resentment. He was not surprised to hear of the success of Jesus, and he said to his disciples, 'No one can have anything unless it has been given to him by God. You remember that I told you I was not the Messiah, but had been sent ahead to prepare the way for Him? It is rather like a wedding; the bridegroom has won the bride, and the bridegroom's friend stands by and rejoices in his success. That is what has happened here. Jesus must become greater, while I shall become less important.'

John continued to preach and to teach and to speak out fearlessly against anything which he knew to be wrong. After his period in the region of Aenon, he returned to the territory of Herod Antipas. This Herod was one of the sons of Herod the Great who had tried to kill Jesus, by ordering the death of all baby boys up to two years old, at the time of the visit of the wise men all those years

ago in Bethlehem when that new star had appeared.

Now Herod Antipas had divorced his own wife and had married Herodias who was the wife of his brother Philip, and John the Baptist told him that this was an unlawful thing to do. 'It is wrong for you to be married to your brother's wife,' he said sternly.

For this Herodias bore a grudge against John and wanted to have him killed. Herod would not do that, however; for one thing, he feared the great influence John had over many of the Jewish people who considered him to be a great prophet; and for another, in his heart, Herod knew that John was a just and holy man and he liked to listen to him—even though John's truthful and hard-hitting words often upset him. So he compromised and had John chained and put in prison, instead, hoping to keep him quiet.

Meanwhile, Jesus continued teaching, preaching and healing, with His specially chosen twelve disciples to help Him in His work as he travelled around the country.

All this came to the ears of John the Baptist as he languished in prison feeling very depressed and miserable. Some of John's disciples were still a little jealous of Jesus and doubtful as to who He really was. So John sent them to see Him, probably hoping that they might be convinced that He was the true Messiah and begin to feel more generous and trusting towards Him.

They found Jesus curing and healing all kinds of sickness and disease. They asked Him, 'Are you the one whom John said was to come, or shall we expect someone else?'

Jesus replied, 'Go back to John and tell him

about the things you have seen and heard; how the blind have received their sight, the deaf have had their hearing restored, the lame walk again and the dead have been brought back to life; and the good news of the Gospel has been preached to the poor.' (Gospel is really 'Godspell' which means 'good news'.)

John's disciples could not deny this, and they went back to John feeling reassured. When they had gone, Jesus spoke to the crowd about John: 'What did you expect to see when you went out

to the desert?' He asked them. 'A reed bent to the wind? A man in fine clothes? A prophet? Yes, you saw more than a prophet; for John is the one whom the scriptures foretold would be the messenger to go before Me to prepare the way. Truly there has not been a greater man than John the Baptist. Yet he who is least in the Kingdom of Heaven is greater than John.' (Jesus meant that the meanest and lowest Christian is greater in privilege than the greatest men in the whole world when seen through the eyes of God.)

Salome

Some time after this, Herod had a birthday, and he gave a great party for all the government officials, army commanders and leading people in Galilee. It was a most splendid affair.

During the party, Herodias's daughter, Salome, came in and danced before the guests, and everyone was delighted with her. King Herod was so pleased that he said to her, 'What would you like? You can ask for anything you wish, and I promise you shall have it—even if it is as much as half my kingdom.'

Salome did not know what to ask for, so she went and consulted her mother. 'What shall I say?' she asked her.

'Ask for the head of John the Baptist,' replied Herodias wickedly, for she had not forgotten her grudge against John.

Back went Salome to Herod and said, 'I want the head of John the Baptist given to me on a dish immediately.'

Herod was very sad when he heard this, for he did not want John killed, but as he had given a solemn promise in front of so many people, he felt he must not break his word. So he sent a soldier of the guard with orders to bring him John the Baptist's head at once.

The guard went and beheaded John, brought his head and gave it to Salome; and Salome gave it to her mother.

Herod's conscience continued to trouble him about this, and no wonder. Some time later he heard about the work of Jesus and the wonderful things He was doing. Some people thought Jesus was the prophet Elijah, but King Herod, greatly alarmed, said, 'It is John the Baptist, whose head I had cut off. He has come back to life.' King Herod felt greatly troubled.

The Story of the Good Samaritan

One day when Jesus was teaching, a lawyer came up to Him, hoping to trap Him with a clever question. 'What shall I do to gain eternal life?' he asked Jesus.

Jesus replied, 'What do the scriptures tell you? How do you interpret them?'

The lawyer replied, 'Love God with all your heart, with all your soul, with all your mind and with all your strength; and love your neighbour as you love yourself.'

'Quite right,' said Jesus. 'Do that and you will live.'

The lawyer, somewhat taken aback, tried to save face by asking another question. Perhaps his conscience pricked him and he wanted to justify his own lack of love.

'But who *is* my neighbour?' he asked, looking puzzled.

Instead of answering directly, Jesus told him a story as He often did when He was teaching. A story is a very good way of explaining a point, because people remember stories far more easily than they remember plain facts and they can repeat the stories to other people.

Jesus's stories had a deeper meaning than most and are called parables, 'earthly stories with a heavenly meaning'. This is the story He told to the lawyer.

Once there was a man who was going on a journey from Jerusalem to Jericho, a distance of about 27 km (17 miles). The way lay along a rocky, lonely and dangerous road infested by murderous brigands.

Suddenly a gang of robbers sprang out from behind some rocks and attacked the man. They tore off his clothes and beat him up, and then left him half dead, lying on the road in the blazing sun. His wounds were very painful, and flies bothered him and he was very thirsty, but there was no one anywhere near to come to his aid. His plight was terrible.

A while later it happened that a priest was travelling along the same road. When the wounded man heard footsteps, he opened his eyes, and when he saw that the figure was a priest, he felt a little happier. Surely here was someone who would help?

The priest saw the man, but he did not stop; he just hurried by on the other side. Perhaps he told himself he hadn't time to stop, as he was on important business for the temple, perhaps he was afraid robbers might attack him too if he stopped so he kept on going.

Sadly, the wounded man heard the footsteps die away in the distance.

Shortly afterwards, there were more footsteps, and the wounded man's hopes rose again when he saw that a Levite was coming that way. A Levite was a helper in the temple, and he might well be expected to be the sort of man who would help someone in distress.

But no, the Levite looked at the wounded man, and then he too hurried by on the other side of the road.

Once more the man heard the footsteps die away and the road became quiet and lonely again. The wounded man felt desperate.

Before long, the man heard more footsteps of a different kind. This time a donkey was coming

down the road with a man on his back. The wounded man was very disappointed to see that the rider was a Samaritan.

The Jews and the Samaritans had been enemies for a very long time. The Jews of Judah in the south hated the Samaritans who lived in Samaria in the north, for the Samaritans were a mixed race and were thought to be not wholly loyal to Israel's God. So the pure-blooded Jews scorned them.

The wounded man felt pretty sure he could not expect any help from a Samaritan, but, to his great surprise, the donkey stopped and the rider dismounted. He came over to the wounded man and looked kindly at him. He felt sorry and wondered what he could do to help. His own safety did not seem to worry him.

Then he went back to his donkey and brought over some oil and some wine which he had with him. These he put on the man's wounds, to act as antiseptic and ointment, and bandaged him up. He probably had to tear up some of his own

clothes in order to make strips for bandages as it is unlikely that he carried any with him.

Next he lifted up the wounded man gently and put him on his own donkey. Then, with the Samaritan walking at the side and holding the wounded man, they slowly made their way until they came to an inn.

The Samaritan asked the innkeeper for a room, and led the man to it and took care of him there. He put him to bed, bathed his wounds with water and bandaged them up afresh, and gave the man some food and drink. Then he made him comfortable and left him to sleep.

The following day the Samaritan had to continue his journey, but before he went, he wondered what else he could do for the wounded man who would have to remain resting at the inn for quite some time until he was well enough to return to his family.

He took out two coins and gave them to the innkeeper. 'Look after him,' he told the innkeeper, 'and if it should cost you any more than this, I will pay you the extra amount when I come back this way again.'

Having finished his story, Jesus turned to the lawyer and asked, 'Which of the three passers-by do you think acted like a neighbour to the man attacked by the robbers?'

'The one who showed pity and acted kindly to him,' replied the lawyer.

'Then go and do the same,' said Jesus.

The Story of the Prodigal Son

There was once a man who had two sons to whom he would leave all that he owned when he died.

One day the younger son went to his father and said, 'Father, give me my share of the property *now*.'

He wanted to go off and enjoy himself and did not want to wait until his father had died. His father loved him and did not want him to go away, but he also knew that the youth was old enough to go out into the world if he wished to do so. So he gave him his share of the property as the lad had asked.

The youth sold it and, with the money, he set off for a far country. Once there, he made lots of friends, because people were eager to know him when they found that he had a great deal of money to spend. He gave presents and parties and generally had what he thought was a good time. He did not look for work because he did not think it important when he had so much money. Instead he just went on wasting his time and his wealth doing silly and foolish things and having what he thought was a jolly good time.

The day came when he realized with a shock that all his money was spent. The people whom he had thought were friends did not want to know him now that he was poor, for they were not true friends and had only wanted him for what they could get out of him.

So there he was, without money, without friends, all alone in a foreign country. Worse still, a famine arose in the country and there was scarcely any food to be had. So, on top of everything, now he was hungry too.

He decided he would have to look for work, but it was difficult to find any as he had never learnt any skill or trade.

At last someone gave him a job looking after pigs, and he went out into the fields and fed the animals. He was so hungry himself, because no one gave him anything to eat, that he would gladly have eaten the pigs' food which was made up of scraps of all sorts of things that only pigs would find delicious.

One day it dawned upon him just how foolish he had been. He began to think about his father and his home, and how kindly he had been treated there. Even his father's servants were well fed and better off than he was, he thought, and yet he, the son of the house, was perishing with hunger in a foreign land.

He decided to swallow any pride he had left and go back home. He would tell his father how truly sorry he was and how ashamed he felt at what he had done. It would not be easy to own up in this way, and perhaps his father would refuse to have him back, but he felt he must try. It was his only hope of saving himself.

Meanwhile, at home, his father had never forgotten the younger son. He still loved him, and although he did not like the way he had behaved, he longed for his return. From time to time he would go out and look to see if there was any sign of the youth in the distance and after a while would return sadly to the house.

As he was watching one day, he saw a figure coming along far off on the road; and while he was still a great way away, he recognized his son! How

delighted the father was! He could hardly believe his eyes.

Wearily the youth trudged towards him, getting ready to say how sorry he was. But the father did not wait for his son to arrive; he ran out to meet him, and threw his arms around him and kissed him.

'Father,' began the son, 'I have sinned against God and against you. I'm not worth being called a son, and I don't deserve to be forgiven. Let me be one of your servants.'

But his father did not seem to be listening. He was calling his servants: 'Hurry up, bring the best robe and put it on him; put a ring on his finger and shoes on his feet. Then go and kill the prize calf and let us have a feast. For here is my son, whom we thought dead, but he is alive; he was lost but now is found!'

And so the joyful party began. There was feasting and dancing and music, because everyone rejoiced that the younger son had come home again safely.

As all this was taking place, the other son, the older one, was out working in the fields, and he did not know what had happened as he had seen no one all day.

On his way back, as he drew near the house, he heard the sounds of music and dancing and wondered what was going on. It was most odd!

He called one of the servants over and asked 'What's happening?'

'Your brother has come home and your father is giving a party because he is so glad to have him back safe and sound,' answered the servant and he rushed off to join in the feast.

Instead of rejoicing, as the others had done, the elder brother was angry and jealous, and refused to go into the house. His father came out and begged him to come in, but the son replied, 'All these years I have worked for you like a slave, and have always obeyed your orders. Yet you have never given me so much as a goat to have a party with my friends. But this wastrel son of yours comes back, having spent all your money in silly and foolish ways, and you give him a grand feast! It isn't fair!'

This mean and jealous attitude of his elder son spoilt the father's joy, and he said to him, 'My son, you are always with me, and everything I have is yours. It was right for us to celebrate and make merry when your brother came back home. For he was lost and is found!'

The father in the story represents God, and in telling the story, Jesus was showing how forgiving God is when anyone is truly sorry for the wrong things he or she has done.

The Stories of the Lost Sheep and the Lost Coin

Jesus told two other stories which show how ready God is to forgive and how happy He is when a sinner repents and goes back to Him.

The occasion arose when a group of tax-collectors and other people with a bad reputation had gathered together to listen to Jesus. The Pharisees, a group who were dedicated to keeping the law in every exact detail, and other teachers of the law started to grumble because Jesus was being friendly to such social outcasts. 'This man Jesus welcomes these outcasts and even goes so far as to eat with them,' they muttered.

Jesus knew what was in their minds, and saw that they were not interpreting the law with enough kindliness. So He told these stories:

'Suppose there was a shepherd who had a hundred sheep,' he began. 'One day he was counting them into the fold and he found that he had lost one, and that he only had ninety-nine.

'What would he do? Does he decide that one sheep is neither here nor there, and not worth bothering about? After all, he still has ninety-nine.

'No; he leaves the ninety-nine sheep safely in the pasture, and goes out and searches for the one that is lost; and he goes on looking, however long it takes, until he finds it.

'Then he is very happy, and he picks up the lost sheep, puts it on his shoulders, and carries it back home. He calls together his friends and neighbours and says to them, "Rejoice with me, for I have found my sheep which was lost!"'

'In the same way,' said Jesus, 'there is more joy in heaven when one person who has sinned repents and comes back to God's ways, than over ninety-nine righteous people who do not need to repent.'

The Lost Coin

The second story was about a woman who lost one of her precious coins.

In those days a woman often wore the coins which made up her dowry in a headdress or necklace. Because they were so important to her, she would consider it disastrous if she lost one and would take a light and peer into all the dark corners of the house, and sweep through it thoroughly until she found the lost coin.

When she did so, she would call together her friends and neighbours to rejoice with her that the lost coin was found.

The Good Shepherd

'I am the good Shepherd,' said Jesus. 'The good Shepherd lays down his life for the sheep.

'A hired man, who is not the shepherd, does not care for the sheep in the same way. He sees a wolf coming and, instead of staying to protect the sheep, he runs away, and so the wolf gets them.

'As God the Father knows Me and I know Him, so I know My sheep and they know Me.

'There are some sheep who belong to Me who are not in the fold, and I must bring them in too. So there will be one flock and one Shepherd.'

The Story of the Sower

Telling parables was one way for Jesus to sort out His listeners. He could tell which of them had come simply for the story and which really wanted to understand the point He was trying to teach.

One of the things which many people, including the disciples, found hard to understand was the nature of the Kingdom of God, about which Jesus talked a lot. So He told them several stories or parables to help them. One of the best-known of these is about a sower.

Jesus was down by the Sea of Galilee when He told this story, and the crowd was so great that He

found it better to get into a boat and push it out a little way. From there He could teach the crowd more easily, than if they were all jostling round Him.

It is quite likely that as He told this particular story, He could see a man sowing seed in one of the fields which sloped down towards the sea. This would make the story more real to His listeners.

One day a man went out to sow. As he scattered his seed in handfuls from his basket, some of it fell on the pathway, which was hard and well trodden by horses, mules and humans. There was little soil in which it might take root, and it was not long before the birds flew down and ate up the seed.

Some of the seed fell on rocky ground, for there were stones sticking up out of the land here and there. The soil was only very shallow, so although the seed started to grow, it could not take root. When the sun came out, the little plants were scorched and quickly withered away because they could not get enough food from the little amount of soil.

Some other seed fell among thornbushes, and though the plants began to grow, the thorns soon choked them and they died.

But some seed fell on the good rich soil, and these plants grew well; they produced lots of corn some 100 grains each, some sixty and some thirty.

The disciples were rather puzzled at this story and they asked Jesus to tell them what it meant. So Jesus explained that the seed is the word of God, and the sower is Jesus Himself.

The various types of soil represent the hearts and minds of people.

The seed which fell on the pathway can be compared to someone who hears the word of God and does not try hard enough to understand it. The birds are like the Devil who comes and takes away the message from their hearts. These people are so busy thinking of other things that it is easy for the Devil to snatch away God's word from them.

The seed which fell on rocky ground, can be compared to people who listen gladly to God's word, but they do not let it sink deeply enough into their hearts. They believe only for a while. Then, when they are faced with a time of testing, they easily fall away.

The seed which fell among thornbushes stands for those who hear, but let the worries and pleasures and riches of the world crowd in and choke the word of God, so that it never grows into anything lasting. These people fail because they try to serve God and the world, and it is not possible to do both.

The seed falling on good ground stands for those who hear the word and let it grow strong in their hearts.

The Parables of the Kingdom of Heaven

Jesus was very careful to explain that His Kingdom was not to be thought of like an earthly kingdom, with boundaries marking its territory. 'My Kingdom,' He said, 'is not of this world.'

His Kingdom was the reign of love and peace for everyone, and could be enjoyed here on earth as well as in the future. But the Kingdom would only come fully when everyone obeyed God's rule. People did not have to build or establish it themselves; all they had to do was to seek it and enter it by obeying God and living according to His laws.

The Parable of the Weeds

One day a man sowed good seed in his field. During the night, while everyone was asleep, a spiteful enemy came and sowed weeds, or tares, among the good seed. These weeds looked very much like wheat and it was not until the ears began to form that the weeds were noticed. The man's servants said to him, 'Sir, did you not sow good seed in this field? Where then have all these weeds come from?'

'An enemy has done it,' replied the man.

'Shall we go and pull up the weeds then?' asked the servants.

'No,' answered the man, 'because in gathering the weeds you might pull up some of the good wheat with them. Let them both grow together until the final harvest, and then I will tell the reapers to gather the weeds first and burn them, and then to gather in the wheat and put it in my barn.'

When the disciples asked Jesus to explain this parable, He said that the field represented the world, the man was Himself, and the enemy was the Devil. The good seed stood for true Christians, and the weeds were the people who belonged to the Devil. It is not for ordinary people to try and distinguish between true and false Christians; that must be left until the end of time (the harvest) when God would sort out the mixture of good and bad.

The Parable of the Mustard Seed

The Kingdom of Heaven, said Jesus, is also like a grain of mustard seed, one of the tiniest of all seeds, but which in hot countries grows to a great size. Here it can develop into a great tree which puts out branches so that birds can come and make their nests in its shade.

In this way each single follower of Christ can sow the Kingdom of God in the place where he lives, and who can say how much it will expand in time?

So the Kingdom of God, which began in an obscure province of Palestine with twelve Galilean disciples, who had neither great wealth nor education, rapidly grew into a worldwide Church.

The Parable of the Leaven

Here, Christ said, the Kingdom of Heaven is like leaven, or yeast, which a woman mixes into flour to make bread; there it bubbles and swells until the whole batch of dough rises.

So God can transform people from within.

The Parable of the Hidden Treasure

Again, Jesus said, the Kingdom is like great treasure hidden in a field. A man comes along and stumbles on it and is so overjoyed that he goes and sells all that he has in order to buy the field.

Selling everything one has is like giving up every sin or self-indulgence which hinders people from living a life wholly for God.

The Parable of the Pearl of Great Price

The Kingdom of Heaven is like a man who is searching for pearls. One day he finds one of supreme value. The cost is high, but he gladly sells everything that he possesses in order to buy that one pearl.

The Parable of the Drag-net

A drag-net is a long net used near the shore, with its bottom end weighted to brush along the sea bed, while the upper edge floats on the surface supported by corks. It catches all the fish in its wide sweep.

Jesus said the Kingdom of Heaven is like a drag-net which fishermen cast into the sea and which gathers in all kinds of fish. Then men bring it ashore and sort the good from the bad. The good they put in barrels and the bad they throw away. So the Church gathers in all kinds of people, good and bad, and of every nation, kingdom and language. The net must be spread wide to include all sorts of people, and at the end of time the sorting will be done by God. Meanwhile it is not for anyone else to decide that a certain person or race is not to be allowed in. Everyone is equal in the eyes of God.

The Story of the Talents

One day a certain man had to leave his home and set out on a long journey. Before he left, he called together his servants and put them in charge of his property while he was away.

He did not leave them all with an equal amount of responsibility, for he knew each man and what he was capable of doing, and so he gave them each a different amount, according to his ability. To one man he gave five talents, to another two talents, and to another one. (A talent was a measure in reckoning money, not a single coin, but a sum of high value. Nowadays we use the word 'talent' to mean a special gift or aptitude; we talk of a gifted or talented person, who can do something very well.)

Having so disposed of his wealth, the man then left.

The servant who had been given the five talents went away and traded with them. He put what had been entrusted to him to good use, and before long found that he had made a profit of another five talents.

The servant who had been given two talents also went and traded with them, and soon he, too, had made another two talents.

But the servant who had received the one talent was not nearly so enterprising. He did not bother to use his abilities to increase his talent in any way. He simply went off and dug a hole in the ground and buried his master's money. There it was of no use to anyone, not even to himself.

A long time passed, and one day the master returned home. One of the first things he did was to call his servants together and settle up accounts with them.

The servant who had received the five talents came and handed the money to his master and said, 'Sir, you gave me five talents, but here are another five which I have earned with them.'

'Well done,' said the master. 'You have been a good and faithful servant. As you have done so well in looking after a relatively small amount, I will now put you in charge of much greater amounts. Come and share my joy and happiness!'

Then the servant who had received the two talents handed the money back to his master and said, 'Sir, you gave me two talents, but I have earned these other two with them.'

'Well done,' said the master, 'you have been a good and faithful servant. As you have done so well in looking after a small amount, I will now put you in charge of greater amounts. Come and share my joy and happiness!'

Then it was the turn of the servant who had received the one talent. He came forward, full of excuses, and said churlishly, 'Sir, I knew you to be a hard man, reaping harvests where you did not sow them and gathering crops where you did not scatter seed. So I was afraid and went and buried your money in the ground. Here is the one talent which you gave me. Now I hand you back what is yours.'

So this servant made his master out to be as churlish as he himself was. He did not believe that his master would accept a small amount of work done sincerely for him. He thought that as he had only been given a small amount, it could not possibly matter what he did with it. How wrong he was! He had not learnt that even the smallest talent could be put to good use.

Naturally, the master was very displeased with him.

'You wicked and lazy servant!' he said. 'You thought, did you, that I reaped harvests where I did not sow, and gathered crops where I had not scattered seed? Why did you not then take my money and invest it? At least I would have got it back together with any interest it may have earned.'

The servant had not thought of that.

'Take the money away from him,' went on the master, 'and give it to the man who has ten talents. For to everyone who has something, more will be given, and so he will have more than enough. But the person who has little will have even the little he has taken away from him. As for this useless servant, he shall be cast into outer darkness, where he will weep and grind his teeth.'

The master in the story is like Jesus, and the servants are His followers. His going off on a long journey can be likened to Jesus's Ascension, when He returned to Heaven. He entrusted His followers with the task of increasing His kingdom on earth by using the different abilities (or talents) which God had given them.

Each person has been given some talent and has an ability to do something; he or she may be a teacher or a preacher, a musician or a writer, or have great wealth which can be used to help less fortunate people. Someone may be possessed of a kind heart and be able to do all manner of good and helpful things to aid others, or be observant and have the gift of noticing where things want doing, whereas many other people would miss them.

No matter how small it may be, everyone has been given some 'talent' and is good at something. It is no good saying, like the man with the one talent, that we have only been given a little and that therefore it is not worth bothering about.

The story also tells us that if we do not use the ability, talent or gift that we have, we shall soon lose it altogether.

Jesus was pointing out that if we use any talent or gift properly, then we shall find that it will develop and increase.

The Sermon on the Mount

The Sermon on the Mount is a collection of Jesus's teachings, which may not all have been given at one time. Most of Jesus's teaching was done in the open air, and we can imagine Him seated on a hillside with the crowds in their colourful robes gathered all about Him. They listened eagerly to what He was saying, for He spoke with great authority.

All that He said was really putting into words the way He already lived. The power by which He lived His life was the same power by which His followers must also live—namely, the power of prayer.

He showed that men ought not to live merely by a rigid set of rules, but rather by looking at life from God's point of view and by considering other people before themselves.

The Beatitudes

'Beatitude' means 'blessedness' or 'true happiness'.

Whereas people think that they must be rich or powerful in order to be happy, Jesus said that the truly happy person needs neither of these things.

He taught that the truly happy people are those who know they are spiritually poor and learn to rely on God; they are also those who are humble and who live as God wishes; those who are merciful and forgiving; those who are pure in heart, and those who are peacemakers.

The Work of His Disciples in the World

Jesus's followers are those who put 'seasoning' (salt) into life, and also those who light up the way for others. The things such people do and say help others to know something of what God is like. 'You are the salt of the earth', said Jesus, and also 'You are the light of the world.'

Teaching about the Law

Jesus said that He had not come to do away with the old law (the law which God had given Moses on Mount Sinai), but that He had come to fill it out, to extend it, and to show that it dealt not only with deeds, but with the thoughts which give rise to the deeds.

Not only is murder wrong, for example, but the kind of angry thought which could lead to murder is also wrong in itself.

Although the old law said 'an eye for an eye and a tooth for a tooth', Jesus said it is wrong to take vengeance on someone who has wronged you. That only makes a bad situation worse. It is far better to deal kindly with the person.

Jesus told people, 'Love your enemies and pray for those who terrorize you.' It used to be said that you should love your friends and hate your enemies. But there is nothing extraordinary in loving one's friends—anyone can do that—one must also deal kindly with those who are not one's friends.

As in the story of the Good Samaritan love, here, is not a matter of feelings, it is a matter of behaviour.

Warnings about Showing Off

Whatever your deeds may look like to people outside, it is what is in your heart that really matters, said Jesus. So do not make a big show about giving to the needy, so that everyone knows what you are doing. When you give help, do it in such a way that not even your closest friend will know of it.

Teaching about Prayer

Similarly, do not pray so that everyone will see you, but pray somewhere privately. Do not use long, meaningless words, but pray simply. Jesus then gave us a 'pattern prayer' like this:

'Our Father who art in heaven,
Hallowed be Thy Name,
Thy kingdom come,
Thy will be done, on earth as it is in heaven.
Give us this day our daily bread;
And forgive us our debts, as we also have
forgiven our debtors;
And lead us not into temptation, but deliver us
from evil.

Teaching about Riches and Possessions

You can choose whether money and material things or God and spiritual things are your main aim in life, said Jesus.

Do not store up riches on earth, He advised, where moths and rust can get at them and thieves can break in and steal them. Put God first in your life, and He who knows all your needs will supply them. You will then have no need to worry.

You cannot put both God and material things first in your life. You must choose one; but where your heart is, that is where your riches really are.

Judging Others

Do not be critical of others when there is so much that can be criticized in your own life. Jesus said, humorously, that it is like a man who wanted to take a tiny speck out of his brother's eye, but did not notice that there was something the size of a great log in his own eye!

Warning about People who Mislead

Beware of false prophets who look like the real thing but are not so. You can tell what sort any tree is by the fruit it bears. So you can tell what people are really like by the things that they do and they cannot deceive you.

Having the Right Base for Your Life

'Anyone who hears My words and lives by them,' said Jesus, 'is like a man who builds his house on a rock—a firm foundation. The rains may pour down in torrents, and the winds may blow a terrible hurricane, and the floods may swell, but the house will not fall, because it is standing firm on a rock.

'Anyone who hears My words and does not live by them is like a foolish man who builds his house on sand. Then, when the rains come in torrents, and the winds blow in a hurricane, and the floods swell, that house will crash down in ruins, because it was only built on sand which slips away.'

He meant that if you live by His standards, whatever storms and troubles come in life, they will be unable to defeat you.

Jesus Blesses the Children

One day Jesus and His disciples were going to Capernaum, and on the way the disciples were arguing among themselves as to who was the greatest and most important of them.

When they got indoors, Jesus questioned them about this. 'What were you all arguing about on the way here?' He asked. But the disciples would not answer, because they were all feeling somewhat ashamed of themselves. However, Jesus knew, without needing any answer from them, and He sat down and called them all to Him.

'If you want to be first and really important,' He said, 'you must put yourself last. You must be ready to be the servant of everyone else. Those are the people who are truly great.'

Now there was a little child listening to all this— perhaps he was the child who lived in the house— and Jesus put His arm round him, and said, 'The greatest in the Kingdom of Heaven is one who is as humble as this little child. Anyone who welcomes a child is welcoming Me. For he who is least among you is the greatest.'

Jesus was trying to explain to the disciples that God's Kingdom has very different standards from the world. Riches and power do not make anyone great in God's eyes. Being loving, generous, humble and forgiving are far more important, and people with these qualities are the ones who are truly great. Such people may seem as unimportant as a child to the world, but in God's Kingdom they are the ones who are the greatest.

Jesus loved children and as He went about He noticed them playing. Like children today, they liked to pretend they were grown-up, and sometimes they would play at weddings or funerals and fall out over their games.

On one occasion some people brought a number of children to Jesus, knowing how He loved them. They wanted Him to put His hands on them and bless them.

When the disciples saw this, they rebuked the people and tried to send the children away, for they did not want Jesus to be troubled by them. No doubt they thought that children were not important enough to claim His attention.

Jesus, however, thought very differently. He was never troubled by people coming to Him, no matter how young—or how old—they might be. He would never turn anyone away.

He did not like the way the disciples were dealing with the children, and He called them back to Him. Then He said, 'Let the children come to Me, and do not try to stop them, for the Kingdom of God belongs to such children as these. I tell you that whoever does not receive the Kingdom of God in the same spirit as a child, will never enter into it.'

He did not mean that people should be childish and never to grow up in their ideas. He meant that they should receive God's Kingdom in a child-like spirit—that is, one of humble, loving trust. This can apply to anyone of any age.

Then Jesus took the children in His arms and put His hands on each of them and blessed them.

Jesus Calms a Storm and Walks on the Water

On the evening of the day when Jesus had been telling the story of the sower to a crowd of people, He said to the disciples, 'Let us cross to the other side of the lake.'

So they left the crowd, and got into the little boat in which Jesus had been sitting to teach, and they began to row across.

The lake was the Sea of Galilee, which lies low about 183m (600ft) below sea-level. All around there are hills, with deep ravines and gorges, and these act as funnels, drawing down the winds from the mountains. From time to time, these winds lash the waters into a great fury, making it dangerous for small boats.

Suddenly, as Jesus and the disciples were crossing, one of these great strong winds blew up, tossing the little boat about and swooshing in lots of water, putting them all in great danger of sinking or overturning.

The disciples were panic-stricken, even though some of them were experienced sailors. They turned to Jesus and found Him in the back of the boat—fast asleep, for He was tired after being with the crowds all day.

It seemed as though the little boat would be completely swamped by the raging waves, and the terrified disciples rushed to wake Jesus up. 'Master! Master! We are going to perish!' they cried. 'Don't you care?'

Calmly Jesus got up and said to the wind, 'Be quiet!' and to the waves He said, 'Peace, be still.'

And there was at once a great calm.

'Why were you so frightened?' asked Jesus of the disciples. 'Haven't you any faith?'

The disciples looked at one another in awe and wonder and said, 'What sort of man is this—that even the winds and the sea obey Him?'

Jesus Walks on the Water

Another time, by Galilee, Jesus asked the disciples to get into a boat and row across to Bethsaida at the other side of the lake. Meanwhile, He sent the crowd of people home and went up on the hillside by Himself to pray.

By evening time, the disciples in their little boat were far out on the lake, and were being tossed about somewhat, for it was a windy night and the sea was choppy.

Sometime between 3 am and 6 am, when they had been rowing for about 5 or 6 km (3 miles), the disciples looked out and saw a figure walking towards them on the water. They were terrified and screamed with fear. 'It's a ghost!' they cried, their voices trembling.

Then the familiar and beloved voice of Jesus said, 'Do not be afraid. It is I.'

Now Peter, confident and enthusiastic as always, spoke up and said, 'Lord, if it is really You, tell me to come to You on the water.'

'Come,' said Jesus.

So Peter got out of the boat and began to walk on the water towards Jesus. But his faith did not last for long, and when he saw what a strong wind there was, he grew afraid—and as soon as he stopped trusting Jesus, he began to sink. 'Lord! Save me!' he cried out.

Jesus reached out and grabbed hold of his hand and said, 'What little faith you have! Why did you doubt?'

Then they both climbed into the boat, and the wind died down, the raging waves grew calm and the storm faded away.

The disciples turned to Jesus in awe saying, 'Truly, You are the Son of God.'

The Feeding of the Five Thousand

Crowds followed Jesus everywhere, for they saw His miracles and heard His teaching, and they wanted to see and hear more. He was becoming quite famous.

One day, near the time for the Passover Festival, when many Galileans came to Jerusalem, a huge crowd followed Jesus up a hillside. Jesus had been hoping to take His disciples away for a short rest, and they had gone to this quiet place by boat. The crowds, however, had followed round the lake, on foot, and many were already on the hillside when Jesus arrived.

Among them was a young boy whose mother had given him a picnic meal to take out with him. Perhaps he had told her that he was going to see and hear Jesus, the great teacher, and she knew he would probably be away all day. But there were few other people in the crowd, if any, who had thought to bring food with them, even to give to their children.

Jesus sat down on the top of a hill, and looked round at the hundreds of people gathered about Him. He felt sorry for them, for He knew they must be getting hungry and they were all a long way from home.

'It's getting late,' said the disciples. 'Send them all away so that they can go into the towns and villages and buy themselves something to eat.'

Jesus knew He could feed the multitude, but He wanted to test the disciples; so He turned to Philip and said, 'Where can we buy enough bread out here in the open to feed this great crowd?'

Philip said, 'Even if they each had only a little, it would take at least 200 silver coins.'

No one had that sort of money on them, for one silver coin was an average man's wage for a day's work, and 200 such coins would be equal to more than six months' wages.

Then another disciple, Andrew, who was Simon Peter's brother, noticed the boy with the picnic meal. 'There is a lad here,' said Andrew, 'who has brought with him five loaves of barley bread and two small fish—but they won't be anything like enough for all these people.' Andrew and the other disciples began to look worried.

There seemed to be no one else with any food at all.

'Make them all sit down,' said Jesus.

So they all sat down in groups on the green grass; there were about 100 people in some groups and about fifty in others, and in their beautifully coloured robes, in the sunshine, they looked rather like flower beds in a garden in the summertime.

Then Jesus took the five loaves which the boy had offered, gave thanks to God, and broke the loaves and gave them to the disciples to distribute among the people. Then He did the same with the fish.

There were 5,000 men in the crowd, not counting women and children, and the disciples went to each little group, giving food to everyone in it, men, women and children.

The wonderful thing was that no matter how much they gave out, the supply they carried was never finished. Everyone ate and soon they had all had as much as they wanted and felt satisfied and contented.

Jesus did not believe in wasting any of God's good gifts, so He said to the disciples, 'Now gather up all the pieces that remain, so that there shall be no waste.'

Each of the disciples took a large basket and went round collecting up all the scraps they could find; and each filled his basket. This meant that, after 5,000 and more people had been fed, there were still twelve baskets of food remaining from what had been one boy's picnic lunch of five small loaves and two little fish.

The people were all astonished, for they had seen the miracle with their own eyes. They said to one another, 'Surely this is the great prophet who was to come into the world.'

The boy who had given up his picnic must have had a wonderful story to tell his parents when he got back home!

Jesus the Healer

Jesus soon became well known for His works of healing and people came to Him from far and near to be cured of their illnesses.

Healing a Leper

One day, after Jesus had been teaching in Galilee, there came to Him a man who was suffering from a terrible skin disease called leprosy. Today it is possible to cure this disease, but in Jesus's day there was no hope at all. A leper had to keep right away from other people because the law regarded him as unclean. No one, knowing him to be a leper, dare approach him, but if anyone accidentally did come near him, the leper had to cry out 'Unclean!' and people would back hastily away in case they caught the disease.

Thus lepers, as well as being ill, led a very lonely life, entirely cut off from human company, except for other lepers.

But Jesus did not shun them, for He never shunned anyone in trouble. When this leper came and asked to be healed, Jesus stretched out His hand and touched him. The leper said, 'If you will, you can make me clean.'

'I will,' said Jesus. 'Be clean,' and immediately the disease went from the man.

Jesus instructed him not to spread the news of how he had been healed, because He did not want people to come and proclaim Him as the Messiah yet; but told the man to go to a priest to be examined, and to make an offering to prove that he was cured. This was as the law of Israel commanded.

However the man was naturally so excited that he told everyone he met, and the result was that Jesus could not go into the towns for a while and had to stay in the desert.

Jesus Heals Ten Lepers

One day, when Jesus was on the way to Jerusalem, He was entering a village when He was met by ten men who were lepers. They stood a distance away from Him and called, 'Jesus, Master! Have mercy on us!'

No doubt they had heard stories of this wonderful healer and thought that if anyone could heal them, He could.

Jesus saw them, went over to them, and said, 'Go and be examined by the priests.'

Obediently, the ten set off, and on the way they looked at one another and saw that all signs of their leprosy had vanished. Their skins were completely cured. They were delighted!

One of them, who was a Samaritan, turned back and went and threw himself at Jesus's feet and thanked Him.

'Were there not ten men healed?' said Jesus. 'Where are the other nine? Was this man, a foreigner, the only one to come back and give praise and thanks to God?'

Then He said to the leper, 'Get up and go on your way. Your faith has made you whole.'

By this He meant that not only had the leper's faith in Jesus healed his body, it had also healed his soul, because he had given thanks and praise to God to whom the glory was due.

The Centurion's Servant

In Capernaum there lived a centurion. The Roman army was divided into 'centuries', each of a hundred men, and each commanded by a centurion. The Romans worshipped many gods, but as this centurion had gone about among the Jews, he had heard about Jesus and he had faith in Him.

For this reason, when his servant became very ill, the first person the centurion thought of was Jesus. However, he thought, perhaps Jesus would not be likely to come to a Roman soldier's house, and so he sent some Jewish elders to ask Jesus's help.

'Please come,' said the elders to Jesus, 'for this man really deserves your help. Although he is a Roman, he is kind to our people and has even built us a synagogue.'

Jesus went with them, and when they came near to the centurion's house, another group of his Jewish friends came out to Jesus, with a message from the centurion. 'Please don't trouble yourself,' they said, 'for the centurion says he does not deserve to have you in his house, nor does he feel worthy to come to you in person. He says that if you just say the word, his servant will be healed. For he says, "I also am a man under authority, with soldiers under me. I order one to go and he goes, or to come and he comes, and if I tell my slave to do something, he does it."'

The centurion believed that, just as he had power over his men to command that something be done, so Jesus had power from God to speak a word, even at a distance, and his servant would be healed.

Jesus was amazed when He heard this message. 'I tell you,' he said to those around Him, 'I have not found such great faith anywhere else, not even in a Jew.'

When the centurion's messengers returned to the house, they found that the servant was well again.

Blind Bartimaeus

Jesus often made blind men see again, and one day, outside Jericho, there sat a blind man by the road-side. His name was Bartimaeus.

Most blind people have a keen sense of hearing, and Bartimaeus would be able to recognize the familiar sounds of people and animals passing by. He had also heard about the great healer, Jesus of Nazareth, and perhaps he thought about Him a great deal.

One day he heard the noise of a great crowd of people coming along the road, such a noise as he had never heard before. He could tell, from the scraps of conversation he heard, that Jesus was with them. He could not see Jesus, of course, but he wondered if Jesus could see him. He decided to call out and attract His attention. 'Jesus, son of David, have mercy on me!' he cried.

People in the crowd scolded him. 'Be quiet!' they said.

But Bartimaeus cried out all the more loudly, 'Son of David, have mercy on me!' Calling Him 'son of David' showed that Bartimaeus had given some thought as to who Jesus really was.

Jesus stopped and said to the people, 'Call him.'

So they called to him and said, 'Take heart; get up, for Jesus is calling you.'

Bartimaeus threw off his cloak, sprang up and made his way to Jesus.

'What do you want me to do?' Jesus asked.

'Lord, that I might receive my sight,' answered Bartimaeus.

'Go your way,' said Jesus, 'your faith has made you whole.'

And at once Bartimaeus was able to see, and he followed Jesus along the road.

A Blind Man at Bethsaida

Another time, at Bethsaida, some people brought a blind man to Jesus to be healed. Jesus led the man outside the village, touched his eyes with saliva, and placed His hands upon him. Then He asked, 'Can you see anything?'

The man was not used to seeing anything and at first his vision probably seemed blurred. 'Yes,' he said. 'I can see people, but they look like trees walking.'

Then Jesus put His hands on the man's eyes, and now the man saw everything quite clearly.

'Don't go into the village,' said Jesus, for He knew that news of His amazing powers could have

started a rising against the Roman occupiers. He did not want that, and it was important that His miracles should be understood along with His teaching about the Kingdom of God which He had come to bring. Only in this way would people see the full meaning of His mission.

The Man with the Withered Hand

One Sabbath day, when Jesus went to the synagogue, He saw there a man who had a withered, or paralysed, hand. (There is a book—not the Bible—which tells us that this man was a mason, who used to earn his living by using his hands; now he could no longer do so, he had to beg, and he felt this to be a disgrace.)

Some of Jesus's enemies were there too, and they hoped that, if Jesus healed the man, they might be able to accuse Him of breaking the strict Sabbath laws. 'Is it legal to heal on the Sabbath?' they asked.

Jesus replied, 'If you had a sheep and it fell into a pit on the Sabbath, would you or would you not

pull it out? Of how much more value is a man than a sheep? Yes, it is right to do good on the Sabbath.'

His accusers did not reply, for they must have known in their hearts that He was right.

Jesus looked at them, feeling both angry and sorry because they were so stubborn and rigid in their outlook.

He turned to the man and said, 'Stretch out your hand.' The man did so, and found it was mended and whole like the other.

Jesus's accusers then left the synagogue and began to plot how they might bring Him down and destroy Him.

The Woman with the Bent Back

Another Sabbath day, Jesus was teaching in the synagogue and there was a crippled woman present. Her back was bent over so that she could not straighten up, and she had been ill for eighteen years.

She did not ask Jesus to cure her, as others had done, but when He saw her, He called her to Him and, placing His hands upon her, said, 'You are free from your illness.'

At once she straightened her back and stood up and praised God.

Again Jesus was accused, this time by the ruler of the synagogue, of healing on the Sabbath day. This man regarded healing as work, and the law said no work should be done on the Sabbath.

Jesus pointed out how hypocritical this was, for the man would surely feed and water his animals on the Sabbath. Why then should this woman not be healed? His enemies were put to shame, but the ordinary people rejoiced at the wonderful things Jesus did.

The Man with Dropsy

Yet another Sabbath day, Jesus was dining in the house of one of the rulers of the Pharisees, when a man who was suffering from dropsy was brought before Him. (Dropsy is a disease which causes the body to swell.)

Jesus asked the lawyers and Pharisees who were there a testing question: 'Is it lawful to heal on the Sabbath or not?' But they were silent and would not answer.

So Jesus took the man and healed him.

The Nobleman's Son

At Capernaum there lived a nobleman, one of the officials of Herod Antipas, whose son was very ill. He was a rich and important official, but no amount of money had been able to make his son well.

When the man heard that Jesus had come from Judea to Galilee, he set out to look for Him, hoping that He would cure his son.

When eventually he found Jesus, he beseeched Him, 'Please come and heal my son, for he is at the point of death.'

Jesus said, rather sadly, to him, 'Unless you see signs and wonders, you will not believe.' Jesus did not want people to believe in Him just because they saw His miracles. He wanted them to follow His teaching, live by it, and believe in Him for His own sake.

But the nobleman had faith in Jesus and he said, 'Sir, come down before my son dies.'

'Go your way,' said Jesus. 'Your son will live.'

The nobleman believed Him and he set off for home. When he was part of the way there, he saw his servants coming out to meet him. What could it mean? But as he drew nearer, he saw that they looked happy, and he knew the news was good.

'Your son is much better,' they told him. 'He is going to live.'

'What time was it when he started to recover?' asked the nobleman.

'At one o'clock yesterday afternoon the fever left him,' they replied.

The nobleman recalled that this was the very hour when Jesus had told him, 'Your son will live.'

After that, not only he, but all his household, believed in Jesus.

The Man at the Pool

Near the Sheep Gate in Jerusalem, there was a pool with five porches or porticoes; it was called the Pool of Bethesda. This pool, with its five porticoes has since been discovered by archaeologists, down below the level of present-day Jerusalem.

A large number of sick people used to lie in the porches waiting for the waters to become stirred up or 'troubled'. This happened from time to time, perhaps caused by the bubbling up of an underground stream, but the people believed that the first to go into the water when it was bubbling would be cured of his or her illness.

When Jesus went there, He saw, among the crowds of sick people, one man who had been ill for thirty-eight years. He was lying on a mat, and seemed to be the sort of person who had lost all 'drive'.

'Do you really want to get well?' asked Jesus, stopping beside him.

'Sir,' replied the man, 'I have no one to help me into the pool when the water is troubled, and while I am struggling to get in on my own, someone else gets there first, and I lose my chance.'

Obviously the man needed somebody to give him encouragement.

'Get up, pick up your mat, and walk!' said Jesus to him. Immediately the man found he could stand, and he picked up his mat and started to walk.

As this was the Sabbath, it wasn't long before some of the Jews told him he was breaking the law by carrying his mat on the Sabbath day—the law was so rigid that even this was regarded as work, and work was forbidden on the Sabbath. 'But the man who healed me told me to pick it up and walk,' said the man. When he was asked 'Who was that?' he did not know.

Some time afterwards Jesus found the same man in the temple and warned him, 'Now that you are well, you must stop sinning, lest something worse happens to you.'

The man then knew that it was Jesus who had healed him, and when he told the Jews this, they began to persecute Jesus because He performed miracles on the Sabbath.

The Deaf and Dumb Man
One day the people brought to Jesus a man who was deaf and who had great difficulty in speaking.

Most likely, this was because of his deafness. We all learn to speak by repeating the sounds we hear, and if this man had never heard the sounds of speech, he would find it very hard to imitate them.

The people who brought him begged Jesus to heal him.

In His kind and considerate way, Jesus took the man away from the crowd where he would be able to concentrate more easily, for deaf people who can hear slightly find more than one voice at a time to be very distracting.

Because the man could not hear, Jesus used sign language. He put His fingers in the man's ears and touched his tongue. Then He looked up to heaven and sighed.

He said to the man, 'Ephphatha', which means, 'Be opened'.

Immediately the man's ears were opened and his speech was restored, and he began to speak plainly without any trouble.

'How wonderful Jesus is!' said the crowd. 'He even makes the deaf people hear and the dumb people speak.'

The Man with the Evil Spirit
One day, Jesus saw in the synagogue at Capernaum a man possessed by an evil spirit. In other words, he was insane.

'What have You to do with us, Jesus of Nazareth?' screamed the man. 'Have You come to destroy us? I know You. You are God's Holy One.'

'Be quiet, and come out of the man!' ordered Jesus, and the evil came out of him and he fell to the floor unharmed.

Reports of what Jesus had done spread to every part of the region.

Jairus's Daughter
Near the Sea of Galilee there lived a rich man named Jairus who was an official of the local synagogue. He had a daughter who was twelve, and she was ill—so ill that it seemed she would not recover.

When Jairus saw Jesus with a large crowd around Him, he ran towards Him and begged, 'My

daughter is very ill. Please come and lay Your hands on her and make her well.'

So Jesus set off towards Jairus's house, and a great number of people went too, crowding and jostling Him on all sides.

In this crowd was a woman who had had an illness which caused severe bleeding for twelve years. She had spent all her money on doctors and medicines, but instead of getting better, she grew worse. She had heard about Jesus, and she thought to herself, 'If I can only just touch the hem of His robes, I shall be made well.'

So she pushed her way through the crowd and touched His cloak, and she knew she had been made well right at that moment.

Now there was nothing magic about Jesus's clothes, but He could tell the difference between the jostling of the crowd and someone reaching out to Him in real need. 'Who touched Me?' He asked.

The disciples were amazed at this question, and they said, 'Look how hard the crowd is pressing around You, and yet You ask, "Who touched Me?"'

But Jesus knew that someone had touched Him deliberately, and He looked to see who it was. The poor woman, who had hoped not to be noticed, now came forward and fell at Jesus's feet, trembling, and poured out the whole story.

'Don't be afraid,' said Jesus gently, 'your faith has made you well. Go home in peace.'

While He was saying this, some messengers came from Jairus's house and said, 'Don't trouble the Master any more, for your daughter has just died.'

Jesus ignored this and said to Jairus, 'Don't be afraid, just believe, and your daughter will be made well.' And He pressed on.

When they reached Jairus's house, there was a terrible noise going on. Everyone was crying and mourning for the child. 'Why do you make this noise?' asked Jesus. 'The child is not dead, she is asleep.'

But they laughed at Him, for they knew, or thought they knew, that she was really and truly dead.

Then Jesus put them all outside and took with Him only the child's parents and Peter, James and John, and He went into the little girl's room. He took her by the hand and said, 'Get up, little girl.' And her life returned and she started to walk around.

'Give her something to eat,' said Jesus, as He returned her to her overjoyed parents.

The Healing of the Paralysed Man

One day Jesus was teaching in a house in Capernaum, where crowds of people had gone to listen to Him, because news spread quickly when Jesus was about.

This time the house was so full of people that it was impossible even to get through the door, and a great number of people were gathered outside too.

A number of Pharisees and teachers of the law were also there. They had come from Jerusalem and from every town in Galilee and Judea, and some of them had come hoping to oppose Jesus in whatever He said.

But there was one man who could not go to see Jesus, for he was unable to walk. He had an illness which left him paralysed, and all he could do was lie on his bed all day and listen to the people going by outside. (Some versions of the Bible refer to this illness as being 'sick of the palsy'.)

This man was unhappy for another reason, and that was because, in the past, he had led a very sinful life and now he bitterly regretted it. His very illness may have been the result of his past sins—for some sins do result in physical illness—so that, as well as being helpless, the man was also ashamed of himself.

However, he did have four good friends who used to come and visit him and bring him all the news. When they came and told him that Jesus was back in town, how the paralysed man wished that he could see Him! But he could not go to Jesus, and it did not seem very likely that Jesus would call at his house.

When the four friends heard how much the man wanted to see Jesus, they had an idea. Why not take their friend to Him? But how?

They soon solved this problem by deciding to take a corner of the bed each and carry him there themselves. The bed was a flat mat, probably of straw or rushes, which was placed on the floor, and could be rolled up and put aside when not in use.

So the friends set off, through the streets of Capernaum, carrying their friend carefully to the house where Jesus was teaching.

But a great disappointment met them when they got there, for the crowd was so great that they could not get through to take him to Jesus.

However, they were undaunted, for they were the type of men who believe that difficulties are there to be overcome.

They saw that the house had an outside staircase leading to a flat roof. This roof would be used for sleeping on in the warm climate of the country, and also for spreading out flax, or clothing to dry in the sun. It could also be used as extra accommodation if the house became too full.

Why not take the man up the outside staircase and make a hole in the roof and let him in that way? These flat roofs were made of a layer of clay spread over reeds supported on branches which were carried on beams. It would not, therefore, be very difficult to make a hole in the roof which could fairly easily be repaired afterwards.

So the four friends carried the man gently up the stairs and put him down while they set to work to make a hole above the place where Jesus was teaching. Then, using ropes tied to each corner of the mat, they carefully let their friend down, right at Jesus's feet.

Jesus looked at the man on the bed, and then up

at the four anxious faces peering down through the hole in the roof. They did not need to ask Him anything; He knew why they had come, and He knew how great their faith was in Him. But, even so, perhaps they were surprised at what happened next.

Jesus looked down at the paralysed man and said, 'My son, your sins are forgiven you.'

The crowd listening were very surprised too, but to the sick man, it was like a great weight being lifted from his mind. Even if Jesus did not cure him of his paralysis, much of which he knew he deserved, then at least he would now feel happier in his mind.

The teachers of the law and the Pharisees who were listening were anything but happy. They began muttering angrily to themselves saying, 'Who is this who dares to forgive sins? No one can forgive sins but God. This is blasphemy.' ('Blasphemy' means words spoken against the honour of God.)

Jesus knew what they were thinking, and He turned to them and said, 'Why are you thinking such evil things? Which is easier to say to this man, "Your sins are forgiven you," or "Rise, take up your bed and walk."? I will prove to you that the Son of Man has power on earth to forgive sins.' By 'Son of Man' Jesus meant Himself.

Then He turned to the paralysed man and said, 'I say to you, get up, pick up your bed, and go home.'

At once the man found that he had new strength, and he stood up, rolled up the bed on which he had been lying and, praising God, set off for home—to the great astonishment of everyone who was there and who saw the miracle.

The man himself could not have felt happier—his illness was cured and his sins were forgiven, and he was able to make a completely fresh start in life. No doubt his four friends hurried down to rejoice with him.

The crowd went home, full of awe, and they too praised God saying, 'What marvellous things we have seen!'

The Anointing of Jesus

One day Jesus was invited to a meal at the house of one of the religious leaders—a Pharisee named Simon.

Simon does not seem to have loved Jesus very much, even though he invited Him to dinner; he did not attend to the little courtesies which were normal when one invited a guest to a meal. The roads of Palestine were hot and dusty, and it was usual for someone—a servant—to wash the feet of the guests before the meal began—or for water to be provided so that a guest might wash himself and be comfortable.

The host also normally greeted guests with a kiss and sometimes the guest's head was anointed with ointments or perfumes. But Simon the Pharisee had omitted all these polite customs, and perhaps had only invited Jesus out of curiosity, not because he felt particularly friendly towards Him. Perhaps he wanted to have a closer look at this famous teacher whom everyone was talking about, and who was said to perform miracles.

During this meal at Simon's house, a woman whom everyone knew had led a very sinful life, entered the house. There was nothing strange in this, because banquets were often public functions; the dining room may have opened on to the street and have been screened only by curtains, so that entrance was quite easy and people could walk in unannounced.

This woman had heard that Jesus was dining at the house of Simon the Pharisee, and so she had come specially, bringing with her a precious alabaster box full of perfume. (Alabaster is a stone which looks something like marble.)

Jesus was sitting facing inwards towards the table, and the woman moved forward, crying. She was thinking of her past life. As His back was to her, Jesus did not see her approach.

She knelt at Jesus's feet and her tears fell on them, and she wiped them dry with her long hair. This was a very generous act, for it caused the greatest shame in those days for a woman to be seen with her hair loose and untidy. Usually women tied their hair back and covered their heads.

Then this woman kissed Jesus's feet and poured the perfume on to them.

Simon watched all this with growing surprise, and felt that Jesus could not possibly know the woman's history. He thought to himself, 'If this man Jesus was really the prophet He says He is, He would know all about this bad woman and would refuse to have anything to do with her. He would tell her to go away.'

Jesus knew what Simon was thinking, and He looked at him and said, 'Simon, I have something to say to you.'

'Yes,' said Simon, 'tell me what it is.' Despite his shock at what had happened, Simon was interested.

Jesus began to tell Simon one of His parables:

'Once there were two men, and both of them owed money to a money-lender. One owed as much as 500 silver coins, and the other owed him fifty. Neither of them had sufficient money to pay back his debt, but when the money-lender found out, he forgave them both and cancelled their debts. Which man do you think loved him more?'

'I suppose the one to whom he forgave more,' answered Simon.

'That is right,' said Jesus. Then He turned to the woman and, still speaking to Simon, said, 'Do you see this woman, Simon? I came as a guest to your house, yet you did not give Me any water for My feet, but she has washed My feet with her tears and dried them with the hairs of her head. You did not greet Me with a kiss, but she has not ceased to kiss My feet since I came. You provided no oil for My head, but she has poured perfume on My feet. She has shown her great love by her actions and so proves that her many sins in the past have been forgiven. But those who have been forgiven little only love little.'

Jesus meant 'It is plain through the little love that you have shown that you have not been brought to repentance through Me.'

Then Jesus turned to the woman again and said, 'Your sins are forgiven.'

Some of the people sitting around began muttering to themselves, 'Who is this man who can even forgive sins?'

But Jesus was still concerned with the woman, and He said to her, 'Your faith has saved you; go in peace.'

The Woman at Bethany

On another occasion, nearer to the end of His ministry, Jesus was in Bethany, in the house of a man who had once been a leper.

Here a woman came to Him with a jar of very expensive perfume and poured it on His head. The disciples were there and some of them felt angry, especially Judas Iscariot. They said, 'What a dreadful waste! Why couldn't this perfume have been sold for 300 silver coins and the money given to the poor? Surely it is wrong to be so extravagant when so many are hungry and in need!'

Jesus did not agree. 'Leave her alone,' He said. 'It is a fine and loving thing that she has done for Me. You always have the poor with you and you can help them at any time, but you will not always have Me. She has done what she could to prepare My body ahead for the time of My burial. Wherever the Gospel is preached in the whole world, this action of hers will be told to remind people of her.'

The Transfiguration

One day, as Jesus and His disciples were nearing the town of Caesarea Philippi, He asked them, 'Who do people say that I am?'

They answered, 'Some say that You are John the Baptist, others say You are Elijah or Jeremiah, or some other prophet.'

'But what about you?' asked Jesus. 'Who do you think I am?'

The group's natural spokesman, Simon Peter, said firmly, 'You are the Messiah, the Son of the Living God.'

'Well done,' said Jesus. 'You are a rock, Peter, and on this foundation rock I will build My church.' Jesus saw in Peter the man he would eventually become, as firm in his belief as a rock.

Some days later, Jesus gave the three leading disciples a special glimpse of His glory to help and encourage them further.

They had all been working hard with Him, teaching and helping people, and learning new things about Him. Just beyond Caesarea Philippi is a high mountain peak, Mount Hermon, which rises some 2,740 m (9,000 ft) above sea level, and it is believed that this is the mountain on to which Jesus took the three disciples, Peter, James and John.

It would be cooler on the mountain, and the disciples would be glad of a rest, and to be alone with Jesus for a while.

Jesus walked a little way beyond them and began to pray. Suddenly the disciples saw the brightest light they had ever seen, and it came from Jesus Himself. His whole appearance changed; His face shone like the sun and His clothing became white and glistening.

As they got used to the brilliant light, the disciples saw that Jesus was no longer alone, but that there were two other figures with Him. One was Moses, the great law-giver, and the other was Elijah, the great prophet, and they were talking with Jesus. Peter, James and John were so frightened that they did not know what to say.

Then as Moses and Elijah were about to leave Jesus, Peter found his voice and spoke up, 'Master, it is good to be here,' he said; 'let us make three shelters, one for You, one for Moses, and one for Elijah.'

Peter wanted to hold on to the moment, for it was good to be in such glorious surroundings. He thought that if he made shelters for them, like the Tabernacle-tent of the old days in which God was present, then perhaps Moses and Elijah would stay. But he did not really know what he was saying.

As he spoke, a shining cloud appeared and covered them, and the disciples were filled with awe. From out of the cloud came a voice saying, 'This is My own Son; listen to Him.'

Then Jesus came and touched them and said, 'Get up, don't be afraid.' They looked up and the cloud had gone, and Jesus alone stood there.

Peter, James and John had seen the glory of God burst through. Perhaps God had let them see this holy thing in order to turn their thoughts right away from Jesus as an earthly king. Or it may have been to give them some extra help and encouragement to sustain them through the terrible time of Jesus's crucifixion which was soon to come.

As they came down the mountain, Jesus asked them not to speak of what they had seen until after He Himself had risen from the dead. They obeyed, but discussed among themselves what 'rising from the dead' could mean.

This wonderful experience on the mountain is called the Transfiguration.

Jesus Cures a Sick Child

When Jesus and Peter, James and John returned from Mount Hermon, they found the other disciples in the midst of a buzzing crowd of people.

When Jesus asked what was happening a man stepped forward.

'I have a son who is possessed by a devil which makes him speechless and throws him down on the ground where he struggles and grinds his teeth. He has been like this since he was a child. Your disciples are unable to help him.'

Jesus asked to see the boy who was brought before Him and was at once taken ill with a fit.

The father begged Jesus to help his son who frequently harmed himself during one of these attacks.

Jesus commanded the illness to leave the boy and never to return. At once the child gave a loud cry and fell down and lay quite still as if he was dead. Then Jesus took his hand and the boy got to his feet, completely cured, and was returned to the arms of his father.

The description given in the Bible sounds like the illness we call epilepsy. In earlier times people were much less well educated than they are today and thought that people who suffered from epilepsy were possessed by devils. Gradually, as doctors and scientists have learned more about what causes this illness, modern medicines have been developed so that nowadays people with epilepsy lead normal lives.

Zacchaeus

In Jericho there lived a chief tax-collector whose name was Zacchaeus. Because of his job no one liked him, and he had become something of a social outcast. Like the other tax-collectors, he made himself a rich living by demanding more money than was actually due to pay the Roman taxes and keeping what was left over for himself.

Zacchaeus, however, must have had some troublings of conscience, for one day, when he heard that Jesus was going to pass through Jericho, he felt he must have a look at Him.

When he knew that Jesus was near he ran out to see; but there were crowds of people on the road who had all come to see Jesus, and Zacchaeus was only a very small figure. Try as he would, he could not find a gap in the crowd through which it might be possible to see the great teacher, nor was he tall enough to see over the people's heads.

Then he had an idea. He noticed a sycomore tree nearby. This was a tree with leaves like a mulberry and fruit like a fig. It grew to some 10 to 12 m (36 ft) high and had a short trunk and wide spreading branches.

Zacchaeus decided that he would climb this tree, and then he would be able to see Jesus and yet not be seen himself. So he ran on ahead of the crowd, and climbed up into the branches.

Along came Jesus, and Zacchaeus peered through the branches with much interest. To his great surprise, when Jesus reached the tree, he paused and looked up into its branches and said, 'Come down, Zacchaeus, because I am coming to your house today.'

Zacchaeus was amazed, almost too amazed to do anything. After all, there were many priests' houses in Jericho; surely Jesus would be much more likely to go to one of them. To come to the house of a tax-collector was unthinkable. Why, Zacchaeus did not even know how Jesus knew who he was!

Surprised and delighted, Zacchaeus hurried down and greeted Jesus with great joy.

There were murmurings and grumblings in the crowd. 'This man has gone to be the guest of a tax-collector, a sinner,' they said.

Meanwhile at Zacchaeus's house, Jesus was doubtless given a meal, after which He and Zacchaeus had a talk.

Zacchaeus was greatly impressed by Jesus, and he began to realize just how badly he had been living in the past. He knew that he could not go on living as he had been doing, and that now he was face to face with Jesus he must make a choice.

He had hardly ever given any money away to charity before, but now, he decided, was the time to make amends. He must also examine his past dealings and pay back those he had robbed.

So Zacchaeus stood up and said, 'Listen, Lord, I will give half of my goods to the poor, and where I have cheated anyone of money in the past, I will now repay him four times as much.'

Jesus was pleased. 'This shows you to be a true son of Abraham,' He said. 'Salvation has come not only to you, but to your family and household today.'

The crowd, the self-righteous people outside, had been critical of Jesus's action in going to the house of a sinner like Zacchaeus. 'But,' said Jesus, 'I, the Son of Man, came to seek and to save those who are lost.'

Mary, Martha and Lazarus

Among Jesus's many friends was a family of two sisters and a brother. They were named Martha, Mary and Lazarus, and they lived in the village of Bethany which was less than 3 km (1½ miles) from Jerusalem.

One day, when Jesus went to visit them, Mary came and sat beside Him to listen to His teaching. Martha, on the other hand, bustled about getting the best possible meal she could for their visitor, for she was a very hospitable sort of person and liked to make people feel at home.

When she saw that Mary was not helping her, she went to Jesus and said, 'Lord, don't You care that Mary has left me to do all the work myself? Tell her to come and help me. I am terribly busy getting everything ready.'

But Jesus gently reproved her and said, 'Martha, Martha, you are worried over doing so much, but only one thing is needed. Mary has chosen rightly, and it won't be taken away from her.'

Jesus felt that Martha would have honoured Him more by listening to Him, rather than by preparing an elaborate dinner. He would have been just as content with a simple meal and a quiet talk with Martha too.

One day Martha and Mary's brother Lazarus became very ill. His sisters sent a message to Jesus to tell Him how ill His friend was for they felt sure Jesus would help.

When Jesus received the message, He did not go to Bethany for two days. By then He knew that Lazarus had died, but He also knew that He could bring him back to life. He told the disciples that Lazarus was already dead, and added, 'For your sakes, I am glad we were not there.' He meant that the disciples' faith would be strengthened when they reached Bethany and saw what Jesus was going to do.

So they set off, and by the time they got to Bethany, Lazarus had already been dead for four days. Bethany was near to Jerusalem and so many people had come out to see Martha and Mary and to console and comfort them on their brother's death. These visits to comfort mourners were always paid with great ceremony for a week after a death.

When Martha heard that Jesus was on the way, she went out and met Him before He reached Bethany. Meanwhile Mary sat in the house the very picture of grief.

'If You had been here,' said Martha to Jesus, 'Lazarus would not have died. But, even now, I know that God will give You whatever You ask Him.'

Martha had great faith, yet she hardly dared say in words that she hoped Jesus might bring her brother back to life.

'Your brother will return to life again,' said Jesus.

Then Jesus said, 'I am the resurrection and the life; whoever believes in me will live, even if he has died, and those who live and believe in me will never die. Do you believe this, Martha?'

Pious Jews believed in a future resurrection and Jesus was saying that Lazarus was a believer and that therefore he was about to be raised from the dead. To Christians, death is not really death, because it does not break the living union between the soul and God.

Martha gave a wonderful answer to Jesus's

question. 'Yes, Lord,' she said, 'I believe that You are the Messiah, the Son of God, who was to come to the world.'

Then Martha went back into the house and said quietly to Mary, 'The teacher is here,' and Mary got up and hurried out to meet Jesus. The people who were in the house trying to comfort her, followed when they saw her go out. They thought Mary was going to visit the grave to weep there for her dead brother.

For three days the mourners used to visit the grave, believing that the soul was still about and might re-enter the body; on the fourth day it was thought the soul had departed and the mourners went home again.

But Mary did not go to the grave; instead she went straight to Jesus. When she saw Him, she fell at His feet and said, as Martha had done, 'Lord, if You had been here, my brother wouldn't have died.'

Jesus saw that she was weeping, and that many others were weeping too, and His heart was touched. He felt a great sorrow and sympathy for them. 'Where is Lazarus buried?' He asked, very kindly.

'Come and see,' they answered.

Then Jesus Himself wept, showing how deeply He felt and how much He understood Martha and Mary's sorrow.

'See how much He loved Lazarus,' said the people; but a few of them wondered why Jesus had not kept Lazarus from dying if He cared so much about him.

Much moved, Jesus went to the tomb, which was a cave in a hillside with a big stone at its entrance. 'Remove the stone,' He ordered. Everyone looked a little startled.

Martha, losing her faith for a moment, thought that Jesus wanted to take a last look at His friend, and she tried to prevent Him, fearing that by now there would be a bad smell, as Lazarus had been dead for four days. But Jesus said to her, 'Did I not say to you that if you believed, you would sèe God's glory?'

So they took the stone away, and Jesus looked upwards and prayed. He thanked God for the miracle, as if it had been already performed, and He offered the miracle as a proof of His divine mission so that the people standing by might believe in Him. Then He called out in a loud voice, 'Lazarus, come out!'

And Lazarus walked out, still with the grave-clothes wrapped around him.

'Unloose him,' said Jesus, 'and let him go.'

The Entry into Jerusalem

It was Passover time, a busy time in the city, when thousands of Jews were going up to the temple in Jerusalem to keep the festival, the great feast which commemorated the nation's deliverance from Egypt.

Jesus and His disciples were on their way to Jerusalem too, but the disciples could sense that this time their journey had a much more serious feel to it. Although they did not realize it at the time, this was the start of Jesus's last week of life on earth.

Jesus was very set and determined and walked on a little ahead of them. The people following were afraid, for they knew that the rulers wanted to seize Jesus, and by going into Jerusalem they felt that He was heading for certain capture.

Jesus took His twelve disciples aside and said to them, 'We are going to Jerusalem where the chief priests and rulers will condemn the Son of Man to death, and hand Him over to the Gentiles (non-Jews) who will mock, whip and crucify Him. But after three days He will rise again.'

He was talking about Himself and what was to happen, but the disciples did not understand.

As they drew near to the city, they came to Bethphage, which was about 3 km (1½ miles) outside Jerusalem, and near to the Mount of Olives. Here Jesus gave the disciples some special instructions. 'Go into the village over there,' He said, 'and you will find a colt (a young donkey) tied up, on which no one has ever ridden. Untie it and bring it to me. If anyone asks what you are doing, you are to say, "The Master needs it and will return it at once." Then the man will allow you to bring it to me.'

The disciples went and found the colt just as Jesus had said, and as they were untying it, the owners asked what they were doing. The disciples replied as Jesus had told them, and the owners said no more.

When the disciples brought the animal to Jesus, some of them threw their cloaks over it, and Jesus mounted to ride the rest of the way into Jerusalem.

Now the people who had been present when Jesus had brought Lazarus to life again had told many people about what had happened. So when they heard that Jesus was coming to Jerusalem, a great crowd went out to meet Him.

The Pharisees were most put out at this, and they said to one another in frustration, 'You see, we can do nothing; the whole world is following Him.'

The great crowd wanted to honour and praise Jesus as their king. Many knew that it was customary to put down a carpet for a king to walk on, and so they spread their brightly coloured cloaks in the path of Jesus to make a carpet for Him, as a gesture of respect. Other people climbed palm trees along the route, and cut down branches to wave or to spread along the road.

'Hosanna!' they cried, 'Praise to the Son of David! Blessed is He who comes in the name of the Lord! Praise God!'

There were crowds in front and crowds behind, so that the whole city was thrown into an uproar. Among the thousands who had gone up to Jerusalem for the Passover were some from far away places who had never heard anything about Jesus. So they asked, 'Who is He?'

'It is the prophet Jesus, from Nazareth in Galilee,' answered the people.

Some of the Pharisees in the crowd went up to Jesus and said, 'Command Your followers to be quiet.'

But Jesus answered, 'Even if they were quiet, the stones themselves would cry out instead.'

As He came closer to Jerusalem, Jesus wept and said to the city, 'If only you knew what is needed for peace! Yet you cannot see it. Your enemies will destroy you, because you have not recognized that God came to save you.'

That day was the first Palm Sunday.

Cleansing the Temple

The next day Jesus went into the temple. Now the temple was, in a special sense, the place of God's presence, although since the coming of Jesus, people have understood that God is everywhere and is not confined to a special place.

In the outer court of the temple, the Court of the Gentiles, there were a number of money-changers working when Jesus went there.

Jews who came from other countries were not allowed to use their own foreign coins to pay the temple taxes, nor could they buy animals for sacrifice with anything but Jewish money. This meant that they had to go to the money-changers before they could play their part in the festival.

Now the money-changers fixed a very dishonest rate of exchange and charged very high sums, even to the poorest people who could only afford the cheapest sacrifice, which was two pigeons.

Jesus was rightly very angry when He saw all the cheating and robbing that was going on within the temple area. He overturned the money-changers' tables and the stalls of those who were selling pigeons, and He drove all those who were doing such business out of the temple. 'My house is a house of prayer,' He cried, 'but you have made it a den of thieves!'

Then blind and crippled people came to Him to be healed and He healed them in the temple. The chief priests and lawyers were angry at the wonderful things He did—while, on the other hand, they had turned a blind eye to the dishonesty of the money-changers.

Some children came in and shouted praises to Jesus, the praises which they had heard others shouting along the road to Jerusalem. 'Do you hear them? Listen to what they are saying,' said the chief priests and lawyers to Jesus.

'Yes,' answered Jesus. 'Haven't you read in the scriptures, "Out of the mouths of babies and children shall come perfect praise"?' And He left them and went with the disciples to Bethany to lodge for the night.

The Last Supper

During the week which began with the first Palm Sunday came the Passover festival which was celebrated all over Israel.

Jesus and His disciples, who were now in Jerusalem, were also to celebrate the festival, and the disciples asked Jesus, 'Where would you like us to go to get the Passover meal ready, for we must make the arrangements?'

Jesus replied by giving special instructions to two of the disciples: 'Go into the city,' He said, 'and a man carrying a pitcher of water will meet you. Follow him into the house which he enters, and ask the householder where the room is where I am to eat the Passover with my disciples. He will show you an upper room and it is there that you are to prepare the Passover. The rest of us will join you there.'

The two disciples went and found everything as Jesus had said.

In the evening of that day, which was Thursday, Jesus and His disciples assembled in the upper room. They did not know it then, but this was to be no ordinary Passover meal; Jesus was about to transform it into the Lord's Supper—a meal which has been continued in the Church all over the world ever since.

When the supper had been served, Jesus rose from the table, took off His outer garment, and tied a towel round His waist. Then He poured water into a basin and did the job which was normally performed by a slave—He began to wash the disciples' feet.

Not long before, the disciples had been arguing as to who was the greatest, and it seems that not one of them had wanted to do the menial act of feet-washing at the supper for fear of being thought less important than the others. So when Jesus saw that none of them offered to do this courteous act, He rose and willingly did it Himself for the whole company.

When He came to Simon Peter, that disciple protested, 'You shall never wash my feet, Lord. It is not right.'

'If I don't,' said Jesus, 'you have no part with me.'

Jesus meant this symbolically—that unless He washed Peter's sins from him, then he had no link with Jesus.

Then Peter, perhaps beginning to understand, said, 'Lord, not only my feet, but also my hands and my head.'

When Jesus had washed all the disciples' feet, He returned to His place at the table and sat down facing them all.

Then He said, 'You call me teacher and Lord, and you are right to do so, for that is what I am. But if I, your Lord and teacher, have washed your feet, so ought you to follow my example and wash one another's feet.'

Again He was teaching them that the truly great people are those who do not put themselves first, but who serve others and do not think only of their own needs.

As they were eating, Jesus said something startling. 'I tell you truly,' He said, 'that one of you will betray me.'

The disciples were puzzled and looked at one another in alarm, each thinking, 'Surely He cannot mean me.' Peter motioned to the disciple who was sitting next to Jesus (most likely John) to ask Him whom He meant. The disciple asked Him quietly and Jesus replied, 'It is the one to whom I give a piece of bread which I have dipped in the sauce of this dish.'

Then He took a piece of bread, dipped it, and gave it to Judas Iscariot. It was Jesus's last appeal to Judas, but Judas rejected it.

'Do quickly what you are about to do,' said Jesus to Judas, and again the disciples did not understand what Jesus meant, for they did not know that Judas was going to betray their master. Some of them thought that, since Judas was in charge of the money, Jesus was telling him to go out and buy what they needed for the festival, or

perhaps that he should give some of their money to the poor.

But Judas, after he had accepted the bread from Jesus, got up and went out into the night through the dark streets of the city.

During the meal, Jesus did something wonderful. He took a piece of bread, said a prayer of thanks, broke the bread and gave it to His disciples saying, 'Take and eat; this is My body which is given for you.'

Then He took a cup of wine, gave thanks to God, and handed it to them saying, 'This is My blood which is poured out for many for the forgiveness of sins. Do this in memory of Me.'

After Judas had left, Jesus spoke again to the disciples and tried to help them to understand why His death had to happen. 'I shall not be with you for very much longer,' He said, 'and you cannot come where I am going. Now I give you a new commandment, that you love one another. If you act in this way, then everyone will know that you are my disciples.'

'Why can't I follow You now?' asked Peter. 'I am ready to die for You.'

'Are you?' said Jesus sadly. 'I tell you that before the cock crows, you will have said three times that you did not know Me.'

'I'll never say that,' said Peter stoutly, 'even if I have to die with You.'

And the other disciples said the same, protesting their loyalty to Jesus.

Jesus told them much else about what was to happen. He would be returning to His Father and preparing the way for others to come to Him too. His return to God would bring them new power through the Holy Spirit; and the Holy Spirit would be with them all the time all over the world wherever they went, not limited to one particular place, as Jesus in human form had been.

Ever since that night Christians have held the service of the Lord's Supper or Holy Communion in memory of that last meal which Jesus ate with his disciples. This service is held on both weekdays and Sundays throughout the year.

The Garden of Gethsemane

Now Judas was the treasurer of the little band of Jesus's disciples and therefore had charge of the money. He had not always been honest and had at times helped himself from the money bag. Yet for nearly three years he had been among the group of Jesus's closest followers, listening to Him, watching His wonderful deeds, and learning from Him. It was sad that he did not live up to Jesus's hopes for him when He first called him to be a disciple.

Some time before the Last Supper, Judas had gone to the chief priests and had asked, 'How much will you give me if I betray Jesus to you?'

'Thirty silver coins,' they said.

From that time Judas kept on the lookout for an opportunity to betray his master. The chief priests and elders wanted Jesus arrested secretly, for they feared that if they took Him openly, there would be a riot among the people.

When the Passover meal, that Last Supper, ended, Jesus and the disciples sang a hymn and went to the Garden of Gethsemane, which was near the foot of the slopes of the Mount of Olives. It was a quiet garden, away from the noise and bustle of Jerusalem.

Here Jesus said to eight of the disciples, 'Sit here while I go over there and pray.' Then He took Peter, James and John on a little further. To these three He said, 'Wait here and keep watch with Me; for the sorrow in My heart is very great.'

He Himself went a short distance further and threw Himself face down on the ground and prayed to God, 'Father, if it is possible, take this cup of suffering away from me; nevertheless, let not what I wish happen here, but what You wish.' And God sent Him the strength to go through with what was to happen.

Then He got up and went back to the three disciples, and found that they had fallen asleep, for they were tired and worn out by grief and worry. Jesus said to Peter, 'Weren't you able to keep watch with me for even one hour? Watch and pray that you do not fall into temptation. The spirit is willing, but the flesh is weak.'

Jesus went back and prayed, and again when He returned, He found the disciples had fallen asleep, for they could not keep their eyes open. He went away and prayed a third time, and found the disciples sleeping once more when He came back to them. 'Are you still sleeping and resting?' He said. 'Look, the time has come for the Son of Man to be given over into the hands of wicked men. Rise up! Let us be going, for the man who is to betray Me is here.'

While Jesus was still speaking, a crowd of soldiers and other people, including some temple guards, came into the garden. The chief priests and elders had sent them, and they were all armed with swords and clubs and carried lanterns.

Among them was Judas. He had given them a signal, saying, 'The man I kiss is the one you are after. Go up and seize Him and lead Him away safely.'

Judas went up to Jesus and said, 'Hail, master!' and kissed Him.

'Do you betray the Son of Man with a kiss, Judas?' asked Jesus. Then He stepped forward and asked the soldiers, 'Whom do you seek?'

'Jesus of Nazareth,' they answered.

'I am He,' replied Jesus, and as He said this, they all moved back.

Then Simon Peter, who had a sword with him, drew it and struck one of the high priest's servants. His name was Malchus, and the blow cut off his right ear.

'Enough of that!' said Jesus to Peter, and He touched Malchus's ear and healed it. 'Put your sword away. Do you think I will not drink the cup of suffering which My Father has given Me? Do not harm them.'

Jesus then turned to the soldiers and chief priests and said, 'Did you have to come out to fetch Me with swords and clubs as though I were a robber? I was with you in the temple day after day, and yet you did not arrest Me there. This is the hour you act, when the power of darkness rules.'

And the disciples all deserted their master and ran away.

Then the soldiers and the temple guards took hold of Jesus, bound Him and took Him to the house of Annas who was the father-in-law of Caiaphas, the High Priest that year, and a very influential man. He questioned Jesus about His disciples and His teaching and all the things He had done which had angered the high priests.

While this was going on, Simon Peter had been troubled in his conscience about forsaking Jesus, and he had secretly followed Him. He went into the courtyard of the High Priest's house, and the girl who kept the door said to him, 'Aren't you one of that man's disciples?'

'No,' said Peter, 'I am not. I don't even know Him.'

It was a cold night and so the servants and guards had made a charcoal fire and were standing by it and trying to get warm. Peter went over and stood with them.

Meanwhile Jesus was still being questioned, and Annas was trying to trap Him into saying that He had started a secret society. 'I have always spoken openly,' said Jesus to Annas. 'I taught in the synagogues and in the temple, where the Jews meet together. I said nothing secretly. Why don't you ask those who heard Me? They know what I said.'

At this, one of the guards standing by struck Jesus with his hand. 'How dare You speak so?' he said.

Jesus replied, 'If I have said anything wrong, tell Me, but if I have not, why do you hit Me?'

Then Annas sent Him, still bound, to Caiaphas.

Peter was still standing in the courtyard warming himself, and one of those present said, 'Aren't you one of that man's disciples? After all, your speech gives you away as a Galilean.'

'I am not,' said Peter again.

Then one of the servants of the High Priest spoke up. (He was a relative of the man whose ear Peter had cut off.) 'Did I not see you in the garden with Him?' he asked.

Again Peter answered, 'No', and immediately the sound of a cock crowing was heard. And Peter remembered how Jesus had said to him, 'Before the cock crows, you will deny Me three times.' Then he went away and wept bitterly.

The Trials and Crucifixion

Jesus was taken that night to the house of Caiaphas, the High Priest, where all the lawyers and elders had gathered together. They did their best to find some false evidence against Jesus so that they could have Him put to death; but they were unable to find any, even though many of the 'witnesses' did not tell the truth at all, but made things up and twisted the facts of real events.

Jesus kept silent, and it was not until Caiaphas asked, 'Are You the Messiah, the Son of God?' that Jesus replied, 'You have said so. I tell you all that you will see the Son of Man sitting at the right hand of God and coming on the clouds of heaven.'

'Blasphemy!' shrieked the High Priest in furious anger. 'We don't need any more witnesses. You have just heard what He said. What do you think of that?'

'He is guilty and must die,' they replied full of rage and revenge.

Early the next morning the chief priests and elders completed their plans to have Jesus put to death. They bound Him in chains and handed Him over to Pilate, the Roman governor who was Caesar's representative in those parts.

When Pilate saw Jesus before him, he asked, 'Are You the King of the Jews?'

'So you have said,' replied Jesus, but when the chief priests and elders made further accusations against Him, He did not answer, but stood in silence before them.

'Do You hear all these things of which they are accusing You?' asked Pilate.

But when Jesus, with quiet dignity, still refused to answer, Pilate was amazed. 'I find no reason to condemn this man,' he said.

'His teaching is starting a riot,' the accusers urged. 'It began in Galilee and now He has come here.'

When Pilate heard that Jesus was a Galilean, and from the region ruled by Herod, he saw a way out of his difficulty. Herod was in Jerusalem at the time, for the Passover, and so Pilate sent Jesus to him.

Now Herod had been wanting to see Jesus for some time; he had heard about His miracles and hoped to see Him perform one. So he asked Jesus many questions, but still Jesus refused to answer and Herod grew angry. He was not accustomed to such defiance.

Then the chief priests and lawyers made all sorts of accusations against Him, and the soldiers mocked Him. Contemptuously, they put a fine robe on Him and returned Him to Pilate again for his judgment.

At every Passover time it was the custom for the governor to set free one prisoner—whichever one the crowds asked for, and at that time a notorious bandit named Barabbas was being held who was sure to be put to death for his crimes.

When the crowd gathered together, Pilate saw an opportunity to free Jesus. 'Which prisoner shall I set free?' he asked the assembly, 'Jesus or Barabbas?'

'Barabbas!' shouted the crowd, for the chief priests and elders had been about among the people persuading them to ask for Barabbas although they knew what a bad man he was.

'What shall I do with Jesus then?' asked Pilate.

'Crucify Him,' they cried.

'But what crime has He committed?' asked

Pilate, and for answer they shouted all the more, 'Crucify Him!'

While all this was going on, Pilate's wife sent him a message saying, 'Have nothing to do with this just man; I suffered much in a dream last night because of Him.'

She may have realized that Jesus was no ordinary religious teacher, and that her husband would be doing a great wrong if he allowed such an obviously innocent man to be killed. But Pilate saw there was little use in continuing to hope that Jesus might be freed, and as a sign that he was having nothing to do with it, he took a bowl of water and washed his hands in front of them all. 'I am not responsible for this man's death,' he said. 'It is your doing.'

So Barabbas was freed and Jesus was whipped and handed over to be crucified. Pilate's soldiers mocked Him, stripped off His clothes and put a purple robe on Him. Then they made a crown of thorns and put it on His head, and placed a reed in His hand. 'Hail, King of the Jews!' they shouted, and struck Him and spat on Him. It was brutal behaviour.

Once more Pilate tried to reason with the crowd; he took Jesus out to them, hoping perhaps that they would take pity on Him. 'Look at Him,' said Pilate, in desperation, 'I cannot find any reason to condemn Him.'

But still the crowds shouted, 'Crucify Him! Crucify Him!'

'Take Him yourselves and crucify Him,' said Pilate.

'Our law says He ought to die because He claimed to be the Son of God', shouted someone, and everyone else roared in agreement.

This made Pilate afraid and he took Jesus aside and questioned Him again, but still Jesus would not reply. 'You know that I have the power to set You free or to have You crucified?' said Pilate, and this time Jesus did reply. He said, 'You only have power over Me because it was given to you by God Himself.'

Then the crowd shouted to Pilate, 'If you set this man free, you're no friend of Caesar's.' That was

enough for Pilate. He greatly feared the emperor and so he handed Jesus over to the crowd to be crucified.

The Crucifixion

Crucifixion was a most horrible form of death. The victim was nailed to a cross and left hanging there to die in agony. He also had to carry his own cross to the site.

As Jesus was being led to the hill of Calvary, outside the city wall, He fainted under the weight of His cross, and a man named Simon from Cyrene was forced by the soldiers to carry it for Him to the place of execution.

Jesus was hung between two thieves who were also crucified. Above His head Pilate had had a notice placed reading, 'Jesus of Nazareth, King of the Jews.'

Jesus was on the cross for six hours, and during that time He spoke seven times.

First He prayed for the people and the soldiers saying, 'Father, forgive them for they do not know what they are doing.'

Then He spoke to one of the thieves who was repenting of his past, saying, 'Truly I say to you, today you will be with Me in paradise.'

Then He placed His mother Mary in the care of His disciple John: 'Woman, behold your son! Behold your mother!'

Next, in great agony, He repeated some words from a psalm, 'My God, My God, why hast Thou forsaken Me?'

Then He said, 'I thirst', and a sponge soaked in cheap wine was passed up to Him, after which He said, 'It is finished.'

Finally, He prayed, 'Father, into Thy hands I commit My spirit,' and then He died.

For the last three hours that Jesus was on the cross, the sun ceased to shine and there was darkness over all the land; also the curtain which hung in the temple was torn in two.

When Jesus had died, one of the soldiers plunged his spear into His side to make certain He was dead. The people who had gathered there went back home, many feeling very sad, especially those who had known Jesus personally and who were still loyal to him.

Among those who remained loyal to Jesus were two important men who wished to see that He had a proper burial. One man was named Joseph and came from Arimathea in Judea; although he was a member of the council, he had not agreed with their decision over Jesus. The other was a man named Nicodemus, who had come to Jesus one night to talk about the Kingdom of God and to learn more about Jesus's way of life.

Joseph went to Pilate and asked if he could have Jesus's body. Pilate agreed, and with Nicodemus, Joseph took the body to a tomb cut in a rock in his own garden, which he had prepared for himself. Nicodemus brought costly spices with which to anoint the body, as was the custom, and they wrapped it in linen and laid it in the tomb. Then they placed a large heavy stone over the entrance.

Mary Magdalene, one of Jesus's followers, and another woman called Mary were watching and they saw where the body of Jesus was lain and went to tell the disciples.

So ended the first Good Friday.

The next day some of the Pharisees and chief priests went to Pilate and said, 'We remember that this man Jesus said He would rise again in three days. Will you give orders that the tomb is guarded until the third day, so that His disciples don't steal the body and tell people He has risen? They could cause a great deal of trouble.'

'Take a guard and make the tomb as secure as possible,' said Pilate.

So they went and put a seal over the stone entrance and left it guarded by Roman soldiers, both by day and by night.

The First Easter Day

The day after Jesus's crucifixion was the seventh day of the week, the Jewish Sabbath (Saturday) when work was forbidden. The following day was the first day of the week (Sunday).

Very early on the morning of that day, before it was properly light, Mary Magdalene and the women who had been loyal to Jesus to the end, went to the tomb taking some sweet-smelling spices for His body.

On the way they remembered the huge stone which had been rolled across the entrance to the tomb and realized that they would probably be unable to move it. 'Who will roll away the stone for us?' they wondered.

As they got nearer, however, they saw to their surprise that the stone had already been moved. St Matthew's Gospel tells us that there had been a violent earthquake, and that an angel had come down and rolled the stone away; the guards had trembled with fear and had 'become like dead men'.

The women crept up to the tomb and looked inside—the body of Jesus had gone! Where He had been lying stood two angels in shining white, who spoke to the women who were frightened and bowed their faces to the ground. 'Don't be afraid,' said the angels. 'Why are you looking for the living among the dead? Jesus is not here. He has risen. You remember that He told you when He was in Galilee that He would be crucified but would rise again on the third day. Go and tell His disciples, and Peter, that He is going before you into Galilee, and there you will see Him.'

Trembling with fear and astonishment, the women ran back to Jerusalem to tell the disciples what had happened. But the disciples didn't believe them and thought that they were talking nonsense.

However, Peter and John decided after a while that they had better go and see for themselves, and so they both ran off to the tomb. Now John was younger than Peter, and so he could run faster and he got there first. He stooped down and looked inside the tomb. Certainly Jesus's body was not there, but the grave-clothes were there, with the cloth which had been around Jesus's head lying separately. Obviously no one would have hurriedly taken off the grave-clothes in order to take Jesus's body away. It was as though the body had simply miraculously passed through them.

Then up came Peter, and he went straight into the tomb. John followed him—and they saw and believed, but still did not understand just what had happened. Feeling very puzzled, they returned to their homes.

Mary Magdalene had gone back to the tomb, and stood outside it weeping. She too looked inside, perhaps wondering if her eyes had deceived her the first time she had looked.

This time there were two angels sitting where the body of Jesus had been—one at the head and the other at the feet. They asked her, 'Why are you weeping?'

Mary replied, 'Because they have taken away my Lord, and I do not know where they have put Him.'

As she said this, she turned and saw someone standing there. It was still not properly light and her eyes were blurred with tears, and so she could not see clearly who it was. 'Woman, why are you weeping? Who is it that you are looking for?' the figure asked.

Thinking that it was probably the gardener who was speaking to her, Mary said, 'Sir, if you have taken Him, tell me where you have laid Him, and I will take Him away.'

Then He said, 'Mary!', and Mary knew it was Jesus! No one else said 'Mary' just like that!

'Teacher!' she said to Him.

'Don't touch Me,' said Jesus, 'for I have not yet gone back to My Father; but go and tell My brothers that I am returning to My Father and their Father, to My God and their God.'

Joyfully Mary went to the disciples to tell them the exciting news. She had seen Jesus! And she told them all that He had said.

Meanwhile the soldiers who had been set to guard Jesus's tomb were terrified and completely baffled at what had happened. They decided that the best thing to do was to go and tell the chief priests just what had occurred—so far as they were able.

The chief priests and elders met, no doubt extremely worried, and decided that they had better try and cover up as best they could. So they gave the soldiers some money and said, 'You must say that Jesus's disciples came in the night and stole His body while you were asleep. If it gets to the governor's ears, we will tell him it wasn't your fault. Don't worry.'

No group of people could have been more miserable and dispirited than the disciples had been when Jesus had died. With their leader gone, they felt that all He had stood for, and all that they had worked for, was now lost. They were without hope, very sad and very afraid.

Peter especially was completely wretched, remembering how he had denied his Lord. How marvellous then to hear that special message which the angels had given to the women! 'Tell His disciples, *and Peter,* that He is going before you into Galilee.'

The Bible does not tell us what happened when Peter met Jesus again. No doubt this was something which Peter would want to keep to himself for ever. But we do know that Jesus did appear to Peter.

Since the wonderful event of Jesus's resurrection, upon which the Christian religion places its firm foundation, Christians have changed their main day of worship from the seventh day of the week (Saturday) to the first day (Sunday), as a reminder that the resurrection happened on a Sunday, the first day of the week.

The First Easter Night

Later on, towards the evening of that wonderful first Easter day, two of Jesus's followers were walking from Jerusalem to the little village of Emmaus, a distance of about 11 km (7 miles).

They did not know that Jesus had risen from the dead, though they had been hearing some strange rumours, and they talked together about the recent and terrible happenings in Jerusalem. How sad that Jesus, their friend and leader, had been put to death! It was the end of their hopes.

As they talked, Jesus Himself came up and walked along with them, but they did not recognize Him. Perhaps His appearance had changed somewhat at His resurrection, or He may have prevented their knowing Him. Certainly they would not be expecting to see Him.

'What are you talking about? What makes you look so unhappy? asked Jesus.

They stood still, looking very sad. Then one of them, named Cleopas, said, 'You must be the only visitor to Jerusalem who does not know about all the things that have been happening there during the past few days.'

'What things?' asked Jesus.

'About Jesus of Nazareth, who was a wonderful prophet, mighty in deed and word,' they answered. 'The chief priests and rulers of the people had Him condemned to death, and He was crucified three days ago. We had hoped that He was the one, promised in the scriptures, who was going to set Israel free.

'But then there was a very surprising report. Some women went to His tomb this morning and could not find His body. They came back and said

that they had seen angels who had told them that Jesus was alive. Then some others went to the tomb and found it as the women had said. But they did not see Jesus.'

'O foolish men, slow to believe all that the prophets foretold,' said Jesus. 'Ought not the Messiah to have suffered these things and to have entered into His glory?'

Then, beginning with the laws of Moses and the writings of the prophets, Jesus explained to them what had been said about Himself in the scriptures. Cleopas and his companion must have found it hard to understand.

By this time, they were approaching the village of Emmaus, and it seemed as though Jesus intended to go on further. But, as it was getting dark, the two followers held Him back and said, 'Stay with us, for it is almost dark and the day has nearly gone.'

Jesus accepted their kind invitation and went in to stay and have a meal with them. As they began to eat, Jesus took some bread and blessed it, and then broke it in pieces and gave it to them.

Suddenly they realized who He was! Perhaps it was the words He spoke as He blessed the bread which seemed familiar to them, or they may have looked closely at His hands as He broke it and seen the marks of the nails. Whatever it was, they knew now, without doubt, that this was Jesus. Then when they looked again, He had gone!

They turned to one another and said, 'We should have known! Didn't it seem like fire burning in us while He was talking to us on the road?'

Although it was late, they got up at once and

hurried all the long way back to Jerusalem to tell the disciples the stupendous news.

They found them gathered together, behind locked doors because they feared the Jewish authorities, but were somewhat surprised when the disciples greeted them with the news, 'The Lord is risen and has appeared to Simon!'

Then, while Cleopas and his companion were telling the disciples their story about what had happened at Emmaus, Jesus Himself suddenly appeared among them. They were all terrified and thought they were seeing a ghost.

'Peace be with you,' said Jesus. 'Why are you so frightened and full of doubts? Look at My hands and My feet. Touch Me, and you will know that it is I, for a spirit does not have flesh and bones as you can see I have.' And He showed them His hands and His feet.

Still the disciples found it hard to believe, although they were full of happiness.

'Have you anything here to eat?' asked Jesus, and they gave Him a piece of cooked fish, which He ate as further proof that He was not a spirit.

Now one of the eleven disciples, Thomas, was not present on this occasion, and when they met him later the other disciples burst out with the news, 'We have seen the Lord!'

Thomas just couldn't believe it and he said, 'Unless I see the marks of the nails in His hands, and put my finger in them, and place my hand in the wound in His side, I will not believe it.' Thomas, like many others, would only be satisfied with the evidence of his senses.

Eight days later, the disciples were together, again behind locked doors, and this time Thomas was present. Once more Jesus came and stood among them. 'Thomas,' He said, 'Put your finger here and see My hands, put your hand in My side, and do not doubt any more, but believe.'

Thomas knew then it was truly Jesus and he said, 'My Lord and my God!'

'You believe because you have seen,' said Jesus, 'but happy are the people who believe without seeing Me.'

Breakfast on the Shore

Some time after this, seven of the disciples were by the Sea of Galilee. The seven were Simon Peter, James and John, Thomas, Nathanael, and two others. Simon Peter said, 'I'm going fishing.'

'We'll come too,' said the others, and they all set out in a boat.

Although the disciples worked hard all night, they did not catch any fish. Usually it was easier to catch fish at night, because they could not see the nets, but the fishermen had no success on this night.

As dawn broke and the sun began to rise, they noticed someone standing by the water's edge. 'Young men,' He called, 'have you caught any fish?'

'Not one,' they answered.

'Let your net down over the right side of the boat, and then you will catch some,' advised the man.

So, despite their unsuccessful and tiring night, they threw the net out as instructed, and to their amazement found that they could not pull it back in because they had caught so many fish.

John then realized who the man on the shore was. 'It is the Lord!' he gasped.

As soon as Peter heard that, he wrapped his coat around him, jumped out of the boat and waded ashore, for they were only about 100 m (109 yd) from the land. The other disciples followed in the boat, dragging the net, heavy with the catch.

As they got nearer, they saw that Jesus had prepared a charcoal fire and had some fish and bread ready for them. 'Bring some of those fish you've just caught,' He said.

Peter went to help drag in the net and, when they counted, they found that they had caught 153 large fish; yet, much to their surprise and relief, the net was not broken, despite the great weight it held.

'Come and eat,' said Jesus, and He gave them the bread and fish.

When they had eaten, Jesus said to Simon Peter, 'Simon, do you love me more than these others?'

Peter had earlier boasted of his great love and loyalty for Jesus, but now, after his denials, he was more humble. 'Lord, You know that I love You,' he replied.

'Take care of My lambs,' said Jesus, meaning His followers.

Then a second time Jesus asked Peter if he loved Him. 'Yes, Lord, You know that I do,' said Peter.

'Take care of My sheep,' said Jesus.

A third time Jesus asked the same question, and Peter said, 'Lord, You know everything. You know I love You.'

'Take care of My sheep,' said Jesus again.

This would not be an easy task, but Peter was to stick to it and help many 'sheep' to come to love and work for Jesus, the Good Shepherd.

Peter was sad that Jesus had asked him three times if he loved Him, but as he had once denied Jesus three times, perhaps this was Jesus's way of cancelling out these three denials with the three statements that Peter really did love Him. It was also a way of restoring Peter to his old position as leader, and of giving him the task of caring for people.

The Ascension and First Whitsunday

For forty days after Jesus had risen from the dead on the first Easter Sunday, He was seen by many of His friends at various times. There could be no doubt that He was alive again and had risen from the dead, just as He had said He would.

Sometimes He was with them, sometimes He was not. He could appear among them even if they were in a room with all the doors and windows firmly closed, for His body was different since His resurrection.

When He came in the midst of them like that He always knew what had been happening just beforehand. Gradually they began to realize that whether they could see Him or not, whether they could hear Him or not, He was always with them and this gave them great comfort.

During this time—sometimes referred to as the 'Great Forty Days'—the disciples listened hard to what He told them, learning no doubt that they would be expected to carry on His work. For He knew that the time was coming when He would have to leave them in bodily form, and they would not actually see and hear Him on earth any more as they had until now.

He charged the disciples: 'Go into all the world and make people My disciples, baptizing them in the name of the Father, and of the Son, and of the Holy Spirit, and teaching them to obey My commands. And I will be with you always, even until the end of the world.'

Now on the fortieth day after the resurrection, He had led them out as far as Bethany and on to a hill. He had given them special orders that they were not to leave Jerusalem until they received the gift of the Holy Spirit which would strengthen them for their great work and give them the courage they would need.

'Are You now going to restore Israel to be a great nation again?' asked the disciples. They hoped He would make the Jewish nation independent of Rome, which was what the Jews had always thought the Messiah would do. They still had not learned that God's Kingdom is not of this world. After all, if He who had been killed and had then risen from the dead were to show Himself to all the people in Jerusalem and to the chief priests and elders and to Pilate and King Herod, surely then they would have to accept that He was truly the Messiah, the Son of God, King of the Jews.

'It is not for anyone to know that,' said Jesus, 'for times and seasons belong to God's authority alone.'

Meanwhile the disciples had to set about the task of winning the world for God—a seemingly impossible job for such a small band of men, but Jesus knew that with God all things are possible, and He said, 'When the Holy Spirit comes to you, you will be filled with power and will be My witnesses in Jerusalem, in all Judea and Samaria, and to the ends of the earth.'

After He had said this, He blessed them, and then a cloud covered Him and took Him up out of their sight.

As the disciples stood gazing at the sky, two angels appeared beside them and said, 'You men of Galilee, why are you standing gazing up into heaven? This same Jesus, who was taken from you into heaven, will come back in the same way that you have seen Him depart from you into heaven.'

Although the disciples would see Jesus no more, they felt happy and returned to Jerusalem with great joy. They were happy because He had blessed them, and full of joy that He would always be with them, even though they could not see Him any longer as they had done before.

Now they could look forward to the coming of God's Holy Spirit which would give them power and strength for the great work which was ahead.

The day on which Jesus ascended (went back up) to heaven is called Ascension Day, and it is celebrated by the Church each year on the fortieth day after Easter (always on a Thursday).

'Ascension' means 'going up'. When we say that Jesus 'ascended to heaven', we do not necessarily mean that heaven is a place above the sky. 'Up' in this sense means 'better, different', rather as you might say you were 'going up' in school, even though your new classroom may be on a lower floor than your previous one.

The First Whitsunday

After Jesus's ascension into heaven, the disciples went back to Jerusalem. They were still afraid of the Jewish authorities who had killed Jesus, so they stayed indoors where they felt safer. Each day after the ascension they wondered if the gift of the Holy Spirit would come that day and they watched and waited.

A week went by, then eight days, nine days, and, at last, on the tenth day something strange and wonderful happened.

Now the tenth day happened to be the feast of Pentecost. Pentecost means 'fifty', and this feast always came fifty days after the Passover. Pentecost marked the end of the barley harvest, when the Jews presented freshly baked loaves of new, fine, leavened flour in the temple. It was a day of rejoicing and gratitude for the gifts of the earth—rather like a harvest festival. Many people from many countries came to Jerusalem to take part in the feast of Pentecost. It was always a very happy and busy time in the city.

Jesus's band of inner disciples now numbered twelve again, for a new man named Matthias had been chosen to replace Judas Iscariot who had killed himself after his evil deed of betrayal on that night in the Garden of Gethsemane.

This band of twelve are known as the twelve apostles—the word 'apostle' means 'one who is sent' (to preach and teach). The word 'disciple' means 'learner'—and all those who followed Jesus, believed in Him and wanted to obey His teachings were considered as disciples, including the apostles.

On this day of Pentecost, the apostles and probably some other disciples were all gathered together in one place.

Suddenly there was a loud noise, like a rushing mighty wind, and it filled the whole house where they were sitting. They looked at one another in astonishment and saw a glowing light split up into what looked like flames of fire hovering above each of their heads. This was the outward sign that the promised gift of God's Holy Spirit had now come to them.

The mighty wind was a symbol of the power and energy of the Holy Spirit, and the flames of fire were a symbol of the fiery zeal with which the disciples would now be able to proclaim the Gospel.

The effect on them was tremendous. No longer were they weak, cowering, frightened people; instead they felt strong and brave and were filled with a great strength. They found, too, that they could do things which they had been unable to do before. When they spoke to the crowds a little later, they discovered that people who did not speak their language could still understand what they said.

The disciples felt filled with such courage and strength that they immediately left the house and went among the crowds of people outside. These included not only those who lived in Jerusalem, but also countless visitors who had come to Jerusalem for the feast of Pentecost. There were Parthians, Medes and Elamites, representing countries from beyond the influence of the Roman Empire; there were people from Mesopotamia, from Judea, from Cappadocia, Asia Minor, Pamphylia, Egypt and Libya, Crete and Arabia. Yet they could all understand what the disciples were telling them about the wonderful and mighty works of God.

Normally the Galilean speech of the disciples would not have been easy to follow. Now everyone in the crowd heard his own language being spoken. They were amazed and puzzled.

'What does it mean?' the crowds asked one another. 'They are drunk with wine,' said others mockingly.

Then Peter, standing up with the other eleven apostles, began to speak courageously to the crowd in a loud voice. It was the first ever Christian sermon. 'These people are not drunk with wine,' he began; 'but what you see and hear is what the prophet Joel said would happen. He said that God would send His Spirit to all.' (Peter was quoting from the prophet Joel whose book forms part of the Old Testament.)

'Listen to these words, men of Israel,' went on Peter, 'Jesus of Nazareth was sent by God—a fact proved by all the wonders and miracles which God worked through Him. Yet by the hands of sinful and lawless men He was crucified. But God raised Him from the dead, and set Him free from the power of death. Moreover, He has ascended to the right hand of God, and has sent His Holy Spirit as He promised. What you now see and hear is that gift of the Holy Spirit which is poured out upon us. It is certain that this Jesus, whom you crucified, is the One whom God has sent to be our Lord and Messiah.'

When the people heard this brave message, many of them were upset and very troubled. They said to the apostles, 'What shall we do then?'

Peter replied, 'You must start afresh. Give up your sins and be baptized in the name of Jesus Christ. Your sins will then be forgiven, and you will receive the gift of the Holy Spirit.'

Many of the crowd believed Peter's powerful words and they came to be baptized. About 3,000 people were added to the group of believers on that day. They learnt from the apostles and shared fellowship meals and prayer.

Because of their firm faith, the apostles were able to perform many miracles and wonders, and more and more believers were added to their number. Baptism was followed by a new sense of community, which resulted in a practical sharing of their belongings with one another. The richer ones among them sold their property and possessions and gave the money to those who were in need. Every day they went to the temple, and had meals together in their homes.

Such was the way in which the Christian Church began on the first Whitsunday. (Whitsun got its name because it was originally a day for baptisms when those to be baptized dressed in white. It therefore came to be called White-Sunday or Whitsunday.)

Peter and John and the Lame Man

One day Peter and John went to the temple at three o'clock in the afternoon, which was one of the set hours for prayer. The temple was a beautiful building, and one of its doors (or gates) was so lovely that it was called the Beautiful Gate. It is thought that this gate was of Corinthian brass and that it was adorned in a costly manner, with much richer and thicker plates of gold and silver than the others.

In front of this gate was a man who had been lame all his life and was unable to walk. Friends carried him there each day and left him to beg for money, for there would always be plenty of people coming and going at this spot.

When the lame man saw Peter and John approaching, he held out his hands asking for money. He may have thought they looked kindly, or he might even have known that they had been friends of Jesus.

Peter and John stopped. 'Look at us,' said Peter. So the lame man looked, hopefully, expecting that they would now give him something.

But Peter and John had no money, and the lame man was very surprised at what Peter said next. 'I haven't any money, but what I do have I will give you,' said Peter. 'In the name of Jesus Christ of Nazareth, get up and walk!'

He took hold of the man's right hand and helped him up. At once the man felt strength come into his feet and ankles, and he stood up and found that he could move around.

Walking and jumping for joy, he went with Peter and John into the temple and praised God.

The people standing around were absolutely amazed. 'Isn't this the beggar who sat asking for alms at the Beautiful Gate?' they asked one another. As the man held on to Peter and John, the astonished people ran up to them. Peter saw the crowd and spoke to them.

'Men of Israel,' he said, 'why are you so surprised and why do you keep staring at us? Do you think it was through our own power that we made this man walk? No, it was through faith in the name of Jesus that this man was made well, and was given perfect health—the same Jesus you rejected in Pilate's presence, even when Pilate wanted to set Him free. He was holy and good, but you asked Pilate to set free a murderer, Barabbas, instead, and killed Jesus; but God raised Him from the dead.

'I know that what you and your leaders did was due to ignorance, but now you must repent and turn to God, so that He can forgive your sins. For God sent Jesus to you Jews first, to bless you in turning away from your wickedness.'

Peter and John were still speaking when some priests, the captain of the temple guard, and some Sadducees arrived. They were annoyed with Peter and John, because the two apostles were telling people that Jesus had risen from the dead, and the Sadducees, in particular, did not believe in resurrection. They arrested Peter and John, and put them in prison until the next day, for it was by now getting late.

Even so, many of the people outside believed what Peter and John had been telling them, and the number of believers grew to be about 5,000 strong.

The next day a full and important meeting of the Sanhedrin (the Jewish Council) was summoned. They commanded Peter and John to appear before them. 'By what power did you make the lame man walk?' they demanded of the two apostles.

Peter, inspired by the Holy Spirit, began to address them: 'Leaders of the people and elders,' he began, 'we are being examined today because of a good deed which we did to a cripple, and you want to know how we healed him. It was through the power of Jesus Christ of Nazareth, whom you crucified and whom God raised from the dead. He is the stone which was rejected by the builders and yet has become the most important corner-stone of all. You can only be saved through Him, for in all the world there is no one else who can save us from our sins.'

The members of the Council were astounded when they heard this speech, for they saw that Peter and John were only untrained ordinary men, but they knew too that they had been with Jesus.

However, seeing the cripple standing up straight and able to walk, they found it difficult to con-demn them. The puzzled Council members then sent Peter and John outside while they held a private conference.

'What shall we do with these men?' they asked one another. 'We certainly cannot deny that the lame man has been healed. All Jerusalem can see that. Yet we don't want their teaching to spread further among the people. We'd better warn them.'

So they called Peter and John in again and said, 'You must not speak or teach any more in the name of Jesus.'

But Peter and John would have none of that. They felt far too strongly to let anyone stop them teaching about Jesus. They replied, 'You must judge whether it is right to listen to God or to listen to you, but we cannot help speaking of what we have seen and heard.'

The Council warned them even more threaten-ingly and then let them go. They knew they dare not punish them, because of all the people who were praising God for what had happened.

Peter and John returned to their friends and told them what had occurred. The believers gathered together and prayed to God to help them to be bold. When they had finished praying, the place where they were meeting began to shake, and they were all filled with the Holy Spirit and went out to preach God's message fearlessly.

Peter and Cornelius

Up to now, the disciples had been preaching the Gospel only to Jews, converts and Samaritans who observed the law of Moses. But God did not want the news to remain limited. So, using Peter and a Roman centurion named Cornelius, He showed clearly that the Gospel was for all men—Jews and Gentiles alike.

Cornelius was a Roman centurion living in Caesarea. He was a good man whose whole family worshipped God; he often prayed and gave generously to the poor.

About three o'clock one afternoon he had a vision in which he clearly saw an angel come to him and say, 'Cornelius!' Staring at the angel in terror, Cornelius said, 'What is it, Lord?'

The angel replied, 'The Lord has heard your prayers and seen your good deeds. Now, send some men to Joppa for a man named Simon Peter; he is lodging with a leather-worker named Simon, whose house is by the sea.'

Cornelius obeyed, and sent two servants and a soldier to Joppa, having explained to them what had happened.

The next day, as they were still on their way and just approaching Joppa, which was some 50km (34 miles) from Caesarea, Peter went up on to the flat roof of Simon's house to pray. It was about noon.

He was feeling hungry and had asked for something to eat. While the food was being prepared, Peter too had a vision. He saw the heavens opened and something like a large sheet lowered by its four corners to the earth. In the sheet were all kinds of animals, reptiles and wild birds. Then a voice said, 'Rise, Peter, kill and eat.'

'Certainly not,' replied Peter, 'for I have never eaten anything common or unclean.' (The Jews had strict laws about food, dividing it into things that were 'clean' and could be eaten, and those that were 'unclean' and could not. They were, for instance, generally allowed to eat animals which chewed the cud and had cloven hooves. Gentiles, on the other hand, ate food which the Jews considered unclean, like pork and shellfish.)

The voice came to Peter a second time saying, 'What God has cleansed you must not call common or unclean.'

This happened three times and then the sheet was taken back into heaven.

Peter's vision showed that Jews and Gentiles were to eat together on terms of equality. It reminded Peter that he was not to despise the Gentiles, nor anything which God had created. Jesus had once said that what goes into a man's heart defiles him much more than that which goes into his stomach—but Peter had not understood what He meant.

While Peter was still puzzling over what all this could mean, the three men sent by Cornelius arrived. They stood at the gate and asked, 'Have you a guest here named Simon Peter?'

Peter was still on the roof wondering about the vision when the Holy Spirit said to him, 'There are three men here looking for you. Go down and accompany them, for I have sent them.'

So Peter went down and said, 'I am the man you are seeking. Why have you come?'

'The centurion Cornelius sent us,' they replied. 'He is a good, God-fearing man, highly respected by the Jews. An angel told him to send for you.'

Peter invited the men in and they stayed for the night. The next day the four of them set off back to Caesarea, and some of the believers in Joppa also went with them. When they arrived, Cornelius met them, and he fell down at Peter's feet and worshipped him. 'Get up,' said Peter, 'I am only a man.'

They went into the house where many of Cornelius's relations and close friends had gathered.

Peter said to them, 'You know that it is unlawful for a Jew to visit or associate with Gentiles. But God has shown me that I should not despise any man. So when I was sent for, I came without objection. Now, why did you send for me?'

Cornelius explained about his vision and ended, 'Now that you have come, we are all gathered here in God's sight to hear everything that He has commanded you to say.'

Peter replied, 'I now know that God treats everyone alike. Anyone who worships Him and does what is right is accepted by Him, whether he be Jew or Gentile.'

Then he went on to tell them about Jesus, and how with God's Holy Spirit, He had gone about healing people and doing good. The disciples had been witnesses of all this. Then Jesus had been put to death, but had risen again on the third day, and had appeared to many of His friends and had commanded them to preach the Gospel to people everywhere.

Peter ended by saying, 'Everyone who believes in Him receives forgiveness of sins through the power of His Name.'

While he was speaking to Cornelius's family and friends, the Holy Spirit came down upon them. The believers who had come with Peter from Joppa were surprised that the Holy Spirit should come to Gentiles, for they heard them praising God's greatness and speaking in strange tongues.

'These people have received the Holy Spirit, just as we did,' said Peter. 'What is to stop them from being baptized?'

He ordered that they should be baptized in the name of Jesus Christ. Then they asked him to stay with them for some days.

Later, when Peter went up to Jerusalem, he was criticized for going to the Gentiles and eating with them.

He explained about his vision and how the Holy Spirit had come to those at Caesarea. 'If God gave them the same gift as He gave to us,' he said, 'who was I to withstand God?'

The critics were silenced, but said, 'Then God has also given the Gentiles the opportunity to repent and to live.'

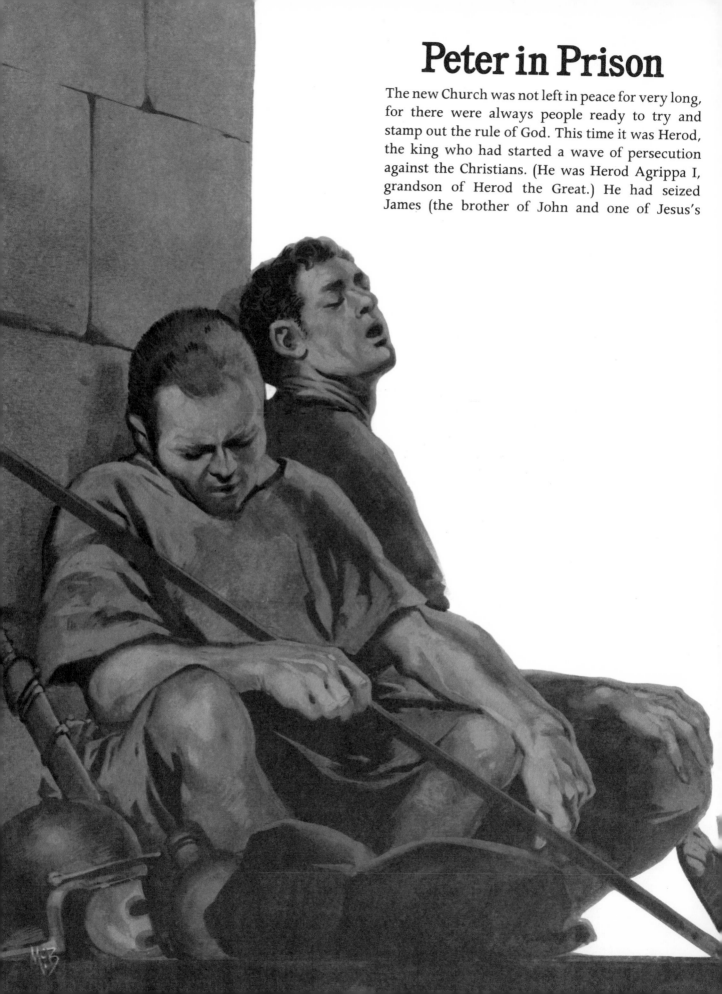

Peter in Prison

The new Church was not left in peace for very long, for there were always people ready to try and stamp out the rule of God. This time it was Herod, the king who had started a wave of persecution against the Christians. (He was Herod Agrippa I, grandson of Herod the Great.) He had seized James (the brother of John and one of Jesus's inner band of three) and had had him put to death with a sword. Then, when he saw how pleased the Jews were with what he had done, he arrested Peter too and put him in prison as well. As it was Passover time, he planned to put him on trial after the festival.

Peter was tied with two chains, and four squads, each of four soldiers, were set to take turns in

guarding him. Peter must have thought that his own days were numbered just as those of James had been.

Outside, however, the disciples were praying for him, and Peter knew that the Holy Spirit would be with him, even in prison and that God would never desert him.

Time dragged slowly by, until it came to the last night before Peter was due to go on trial. Tomorrow Herod would almost certainly have him killed.

Suddenly Peter started. Someone was shaking him by the shoulder and he heard a voice saying, 'Get up quickly!' It was an angel, who had appeared in his cell.

The chains fell from Peter's hands, and the angel said, 'Dress yourself and put on your sandals, wrap your cloak around you and follow me as quickly as possible.'

Peter could hardly believe this was happening; he thought he was dreaming and that, when he awoke, the chains would be there just as firmly as they had been before. But he followed the angel, past the first guard post, then the second, until they came to the great iron gate which led from the prison into the city. Now, surely he would wake up, but, no, the iron gate swung open of its own accord, and out they went into the dark and silent street.

Then the angel disappeared, and Peter realized that it wasn't a dream after all. The wonderful event was true!

No doubt he wondered what would happen when his escape was discovered; soldiers would be sent out to search the city until he was found. He decided he had better take refuge in a friend's house, and he went to the home of Mary, the mother of one of Peter's friends named John Mark. A company of his friends had gathered there to pray for Peter, and doubtless they had been praying very late that night, because they knew that on the morrow Peter would be brought to trial before King Herod.

Peter knocked at the door—not too loudly, for fear there were any enemies about. The friends inside were nervous, wondering whether some more of Herod's soldiers had come to arrest them and drag them off to prison too.

A servant-girl named Rhoda came to the door. She knew better than to open it straightaway, for it may well have been an enemy outside. When she recognized Peter's voice, she was absolutely delighted—so much so that she forgot to open the door and ran back instead to tell the others about it. 'It's Peter!' she cried.

'No! You're crazy!' they said, and refused to believe her.

'But it is Peter,' insisted Rhoda.

'It must be his angel,' they answered.

All this time Peter continued to knock on the door, until at last one of his friends went to open it. They were all overjoyed and amazed when they found that it really was Peter.

Peter put up his hand to motion them to be quiet, and then he explained to them how the angel had come and how he had been able to walk out of the prison. The friends knew that God had indeed answered their prayers.

Peter said that the friends should tell the other believers about the wonderful happenings of that night, but that he must leave them and go somewhere else for safety. Herod's soldiers would almost certainly think of looking for him in the houses of his friends; and, if discovered, that would mean danger for them too.

Peter knew that wherever he went, God would be with him, and that his friends would be praying to ask God to guide him through any difficulties which he might meet.

The next morning, when it was discovered that Peter was missing, there was tremendous confusion among the guards. Herod gave orders for a search party to go out, but they did not find Peter. How he had managed to escape was a complete mystery to them.

Herod, however, was very angry about the whole affair. He had the guards questioned, and when they could give no satisfactory answer, he ordered them to be put to death in a fit of rage and wickedness.

Stephen the Martyr

The Christian Church continued spreading, so much so that the apostles found that there was more work than the twelve of them could do. As well as the preaching and teaching, and the important need for prayer, there was the work of sharing and helping the needy.

It was some complaints from the Greek-speaking Jews which really brought matters to a head; they said that their widows were being neglected.

So the twelve apostles summoned a meeting of the disciples and said, 'It is not right for us to leave off preaching God's word in order to deal with money and food-sharing. We propose that you choose seven men from among you to be put in charge of the sharing; then we twelve can give our full time to prayer and preaching.'

The meeting set about choosing seven new helpers. They were named Philip, Prochorus, Nicanor, Timon, Parmenas, Nicolaus and Stephen.

One of them, Stephen, performed great miracles and wonders, but there were some religious leaders who were very much against Stephen and they argued with him; although they could not deny that he spoke with great wisdom. So, secretly, they produced some men to say that they had heard Stephen speak blasphemous words against God and against Moses. This was completely untrue, but, in this way, they managed to stir up the people. Stephen was arrested and brought before the Council.

There they brought in some false witnesses to tell lies about him and to exaggerate and twist what he had said. 'This man,' they lied, 'is always speaking against the temple and the Law. We've heard him say that Jesus of Nazareth will destroy this place and change the customs of Moses.'

The men sitting in the Council looked at Stephen, expecting a denial, but there was neither anger nor fear in his expression. Instead his face looked like that of an angel. The High Priest asked, 'Is it true?'

Stephen made a long speech in reply. First he told them the history of the Jews, beginning with Abraham and Moses and reminded them how God had delivered the Jews out of the bondage of Egypt; and how the Israelites had turned away from God and had worshipped a golden calf instead. He spoke of David and of Solomon and ended by saying that Israel of old had rejected the prophets, and now they had betrayed and murdered the Messiah Himself.

'You are deaf to God's message, just as your ancestors were. You are the ones who received God's law, yet you are the ones who disobey it.'

When the Council heard these things, they were furious, but Stephen gazed towards heaven and said, 'I see heaven opened and the Son of Man at the right hand of God.'

The Council shouted angrily, covering their ears with their hands at what they considered to be blasphemy. They rushed on Stephen and dragged him out of the city to stone him, leaving their cloaks in the charge of a young man named Saul.

As they were stoning Stephen, he prayed, 'Lord Jesus, receive my spirit.' He knelt down and prayed for his tormentors, crying out, 'Lord, do not hold this sin against them.' Then he died.

Saul, who was in charge of the cloaks, approved of his murder, yet he was to become a very important figure in the life of the Church in the days to come.

The Road to Damascus

The young man named Saul, who had been in charge of the cloaks of those who had stoned Stephen, was born in the city of Tarsus in the south of Asia Minor. He had had a good education, being a clever boy, and had studied in Jerusalem under a famous teacher called Gamaliel.

He grew up to be a firm upholder of the law and a hater of the teaching of Jesus of Nazareth. He resolved to do all in his power to stamp out this new religion and, in raging fury, he sought out Jesus's followers and persecuted them whenever he found them. Not only did he have many of them shut up in prison, but he readily voted against them when they were ordered to be put to death.

One day he was on his way to Damascus, the capital city of Syria, to seek out and arrest the believers there. He had been given letters of introduction to the synagogues in Damascus, so that if he found any of the followers of Jesus there, he could bring them back, bound, to Jerusalem.

Full of threats and hate, he journeyed to Damascus in the company of a group of other men. Suddenly, as they were approaching the city, a brilliant blinding light, brighter than the sun, stopped them in their tracks.

Saul fell to the ground and, as he did so, he heard a voice saying, 'Saul! Saul! Why are you persecuting Me?'

'Who are You, Lord?' asked Saul.

'I am Jesus whom you are persecuting,' came the reply. 'Get up and go into the city, and there you will be told what to do.'

The men who were travelling with Saul were astonished, for they could hear the voice but could not see anyone speaking. They themselves were speechless.

Saul got up from the ground and found that when he opened his eyes he could not see anything. He was blind.

His companions took him by the hand and led

him into Damascus, where for three days he was unable to see and did not eat or drink anything.

Now in Damascus there was a disciple named Ananias, and he had a vision in which the Lord spoke to him. 'Ananias!'

'Here I am, Lord,' replied Ananias.

'Get up and go to the house of a man named Judas in Straight Street, and there ask for a man called Saul from Tarsus. He is praying and in a vision he has seen a man named Ananias come and place his hands on him so that his sight may be restored.'

Ananias was troubled when he heard this and he said, 'But Lord, I have heard about this man and of all the terrible things he has done to Your followers in Jerusalem; and here he has authority from the chief priests to arrest and bind any believers he can find.'

Ananias could not believe that God would want this man; but God knew how Saul would change. 'Go,' He said, 'for he is the man I have chosen to make My name known to the Gentiles and the kings and people of Israel. He will suffer much for the sake of My name.'

So Ananias went to the house in Straight Street where Saul was staying. Obedient to God's will, he placed his hands on him and said, 'Brother Saul, the Lord Jesus, who appeared to you on the road as you were coming, has sent me so that your sight may be restored and that you might be filled with the Holy Spirit.'

Immediately it seemed as though scales fell from Saul's eyes and he found that he could see again.

'Why wait any longer?' said Ananias. 'Be baptized and wash away your sins and call on the name of Jesus.'

Saul got up and he was baptized, and from that time became an unswerving follower of Jesus.

This was a great turning-point in the history of the early Church; from being a violent enemy of the way of Christ, Saul turned about completely and became one of the Church's most ardent leaders. He soon became known as Paul, which was his Roman name and is the name by which he is more familiarly known.

He stayed a few days in Damascus and went into the synagogue and began to preach that Jesus was the Son of God. The disciples in Damascus were amazed. Here was the man who had come to arrest and imprison them actually preaching that they must believe and follow Jesus.

The Jews were furious when they found that this energetic hater of Jesus had now gone over to Jesus's way of life, so they had a meeting and made plans to kill him.

They watched the city gates all day and all night in order to catch Paul if he were to go out of the city. His life was certainly in danger, just as the lives of the believers had been when the old Saul had been persecuting them.

However, Paul's friends discovered the plot and determined to find a way for him to escape. One night, under cover of darkness, they put him in a big basket and lowered him over the city wall. Thus he was able to return safely to Jerusalem.

As soon as he returned to Jerusalem, Paul tried to join the disciples there. Somewhat naturally, they were all afraid of him and could not believe that he had now become one of Jesus's disciples. They suspected he might be using his new life as a trick to arrest them.

One of them, however, a man named Barnabas, believed Paul and he brought him to the apostles and told them how he had been converted on the road to Damascus, and how at Damascus he had preached boldly in the name of Jesus.

Now Paul went all over Jerusalem preaching in Jesus's name, but there were still some Greek-speaking Jews who were against him and wanted to kill him; and when the believers found out about this, they sent Paul back to Tarsus for a while for his own safety.

Paul's First Missionary Journey

Some time later Barnabas went to Tarsus to look for Paul. When he found him, he brought him to Antioch in Syria, and for a year the two men met believers and taught many people. It was at Antioch that the believers were first called 'Christians'.

The group was worshipping one day in Antioch, when they felt that the Holy Spirit was urging them to send Paul and Barnabas to take the message of God's good news to other lands. So they fasted and prayed with them and sent them off on their way to carry Jesus's message.

They set off from Seleucia, which was on the coast, about 26 km (16 miles) from Antioch, and sailed across the sea to the island of Cyprus. There they preached at Salamis and at Paphos, which was the seat of government. The governor of the island, Sergius Paulus, summoned them before him because he wanted to hear why they had come and what they had to say.

At the court there was a false prophet, a sorcerer named Elymas. He was a friend of the governor's and tried to stop the governor from hearing about the true faith. But Paul looked hard at Elymas and said, 'You are a son of the Devil, and the enemy of everything that is good. By your evil tricks you keep trying to distort the truth of God. Now you will be blinded and unable to see anything at all for a time.'

Immediately the false prophet felt mist and darkness come upon his eyes and had to get people to lead him about by the hand. Thus his evil ways were overcome, and the governor became a believer and was astonished at the wonderful teaching about God.

When Paul and his companions left Cyprus they sailed to the mainland where they went to Perga and thence to Antioch in Pisidia (not the same town as Antioch in Syria from which they had started their journey).

Here, at Antioch in Pisidia, they were invited to speak to the people and to give them a message of encouragement. So Paul told them about the great nation of Israel, about how God brought them out of bondage in Egypt, and about Samuel, David and John the Baptist.

Then, addressing both Jews and the Gentiles who worshipped God, he said that it was to all that the message of salvation had been sent, through Jesus's death and resurrection.

The people invited Paul and Barnabas to come back the next Sabbath and tell them more. They did so, and nearly everyone in the town came to hear them. Some Jews, however, were jealous—perhaps because the message was addressed to the Gentiles as well as to themselves, and they contradicted Paul and insulted him and called him a liar.

'The message came to you Jews first,' said Paul and Barnabas even more boldly, 'but you rejected it and so we turned to the Gentiles. For God has set us to be light to the Gentiles and to bring salvation to the whole world.'

The Gentiles were pleased to hear this, but the Jews started a persecution against Paul and Barnabas and drove them out of the district. Undaunted, Paul and Barnabas shook the dust off their feet, and travelled on to Iconium, where their reception was much the same. A great many Jews and Gentiles became believers, but some, both

Jews and Gentiles, were against the apostles and decided to stone them out of the city. When Paul and Barnabas learnt about it, they fled southwards to the cities of Lystra and Derbe.

In Lystra there was a crippled man who had never walked in his life. He sat there, listening intently to Paul's words, and Paul could see that he had great faith. So he said to the man in a loud voice, 'Stand up on your feet!' And the man leapt up and started to walk around, quite overjoyed at the change which had come over him.

When the crowds saw this, they were amazed, and said in their own Lycaonian language, 'The gods have become like men and have come down to us.' They called Barnabas Zeus and Paul Hermes because he was the chief speaker. The priest of Zeus brought bulls and garlands and wanted to offer sacrifice with the people. Paul and Barnabas were not at all pleased at this, and they ran out into the crowd shouting, 'Why are you doing this? We aren't gods—we are humans like you! We have come to bring you good news. You should turn away from idols and worship the real, living God who made heaven and earth and sea, and all that is in them. He sends the rain and the crops to grow at the right time, and so gives you food and happiness.'

Even with these words, Paul and Barnabas were hard put to it to stop the crowds from offering a sacrifice to them.

Then some Jews from Antioch in Pisidia and from Iconium arrived and stirred up the people; they stoned Paul and dragged him out of the city, thinking that he was dead, but the believers came and gathered round him, to protect and help him, and he recovered.

The next day he and Barnabas travelled some 40 km (25 miles) to Derbe. There they made many disciples, and then they started on their return journey home. They went through Lystra, Iconium and Antioch in Pisidia, and were not afraid to go back to places where there were enemies of the faith. They strengthened the Christians and encouraged them to remain true to God, no matter what trials and tribulations might come. Paul himself certainly set a fine example in this no matter what danger he faced.

In each church they appointed elders to look after the new Christians and to continue God's work, and finally they sailed back to Syria and arrived in Antioch in Syria from whence they had started.